"Financial Basics *is a must-read for every college-bound student who wishes to avoid the disastrous pitfalls that have claimed so many. By sharing the stories of real students, Susan Knox has gone well beyond describing financial hazards. She has arrived at real solutions."*

– K. J. (Gus) Kravas, Ph.D.,
Vice Provost for Student Relations, University of Washington

"This book is a must-have for all incoming freshmen or for anyone who wants to finally learn the true basics of personal finance. By sharing her story and stories of others, Susan Knox has made the journey in successful money management real and understandable."

– Anne H. Chasser, Commissioner,
United States Patent and Trademark Office

"Financial Basics *has the potential to make an enormous difference in the lives of college students. Research shows that financial problems present some of the biggest obstacles students face in achieving academic success, or even being able to stay in school. Ms. Knox has written a very helpful and accessible guide; it should be required reading for everyone heading off to college. Or for that matter, for anyone who's finding that money problems are tripping them up in their efforts to live effective lives."*

– Martha Garland, Dean of Accademic Affairs,
The Ohio State University

"Susan has put in this book both the practical and the emotional elements related to credit card debt. Her style and incredible insight give an immediate 'This is me and why didn't someone tell me this before?' reaction from her readers. We intend to use Susan's book as part of our counselor training."

– Cuba Craig, President and CEO,
American Financial Solutions

"Whoever said a CPA can't write for a general audience, especially a young one? They're wrong. Susan Knox has hit a home run. The personal stories draw the reader in, we can all relate to every mistake we, our kids, our students or friends ever made. Each chapter and paragraph is relevant and important. I especially like the way Chapter 13 ties it all together. Doing what Knox suggests can be a life-changing event."

– David A. Lieberman, Senior Vice President
for Business & Finance, University of Miami

"After graduating from college I watched my credit card debt grow each month as I learned to deal with a new set of responsibilities. I felt out of control, with no idea how to manage money. I read many books on the subject. Susan Knox's guide is the only one that really made sense to me. The stories are engaging. The tips are easy to understand and achievable. Her book gave me the tools I needed to feel powerful about my finances. Now, two years later I am debt free and building a solid future thanks to Financial Basics."

– Julie Stonefelt,
The Evergreen State College, class of 2001

"The summer before my senior year at Ohio State, Susan Knox asked me to review her manuscript on Financial Planning for College Students. The book contained so much valuable information, in addition to helpful hints, money management, credit and saving strategies . . . it was exactly what I needed to learn about being a smart personal financial manager. My only regret was that I didn't have all this important information when I started college! I would have made much better financial decisions during my four years at Ohio State."

– Katie Chasser Coakley,
The Ohio State University, class of 2003

FINANCIAL BASICS

FINANCIAL BASICS

A Money-Management Guide for Students

SUSAN KNOX

THE OHIO STATE UNIVERSITY PRESS · *Columbus*

Knox, Susan.
Financial basics : a money-management guide for students / Susan Knox.
    p. cm.
Includes index.
ISBN 0-8142-0978-5 (cloth : alk. paper) — ISBN 0-8142-5130-7 (pbk. : alk. paper)
1. College students—United States—Finance, Personal. I. Title.

   LB2343.32.K66 2004
   332.024'00835—dc22

                            2004003520

Cover design by Dan O'Dair.
Text design by Jennifer Forsythe. Type set in Adobe Palantino.
Printed by Thomson-Shore, Inc.

The paper used in this publication meets the minimum requirements of the American
National Standard for Information Sciences—Permanence of Paper for Printed Library
Materials. ANSI Z39.48–1992.

9 8 7 6 5 4 3 2

In memory of Alan

Contents

Acknowledgments   xiii

Introduction   xv

1 Seduced by Credit Cards
Don't let easy access to credit cards lead to expensive debt as you pay twice as much for your purchases.   1

2 Nervous Breakdown Budget
How to get a handle on your financial needs by creating a realistic spending plan and begin to understand your financial nature and personal spending pattern.   15

3 First in the Family
Learn to think in creative ways to fund your college education and seek out experienced help.   28

4 The Simple Things in Life
Basic money-management facts of life that no one ever tells you.   37

5 Spend, Spend, Spend
The pitfalls of trying to keep up with others who have more money and how ignoring the rules for debt and student loans can change your life.   52

6   How Much Did You Say I Owed?
     Ways to determine how much you can safely afford to borrow for your
     education, being smart about choosing your loan package, and the
     consequences of dropping out of school.   61

7   But Don't I Need to Build a Credit History?
     Basic facts on building credit history and how to ensure that you leave
     college with a good credit rating.   70

8   Car Crazy
     How to make decisions on acquiring those extra things you want
     to buy for college.   79

9   I'll Think about It Tomorrow
     The dangers of ignoring financial responsibility and how to cope with
     the habit of procrastination.   88

10   Now Where Did I Put That?
     What to save, how to store documents, and security issues for your
     sensitive financial information.   95

11   What's Next?
     Financial planning for life after school.   104

12   Develop a Personal Philosophy of Money
     Begin to develop your personal philosophy of money.   114

13   Your Story
     Write about your money management experiences as a way to pinpoint
     your strengths and weaknesses around money.   120

Glossary of Financial Terms   133
Index   141

Acknowledgments

THANKS TO ALL the students and administrators who freely gave their time and personal information for this project. Special thanks to Natala Hart and Carla Mattmiller, The Ohio State University; Jim White, Seattle University; David Lieberman and his staff, University of Miami; Bob Baker, Eric Godfrey, Gene Magallanes, Sandie Roskoe, and Ruth Johnston and her staff, University of Washington; Jaime Coulson, University of Colorado; Janet Gibbs and her staff, Loyola University; Amy Kweskin, Washington University; Paola Di Domenico, Northwestern University; Janet Abraham, formerly at Whittier College; and my sister, Nancy Dominick, Wittenburg University.

I thank The Ohio State University Press: Heather Lee Miller, Malcolm Litchfield, Eugene O'Connor, and Laurie Avery for their support and assistance in making *Financial Basics* a reality.

My heartfelt gratitude to Priscilla Long, Nick O'Connell, Phyllis Hatfield, Suzanne Murray, Brenda Peterson, my classmates in Brenda's class, Laurel Richardson, Alice Acheson, and especially Geri Gale, who instructed and nurtured me in creating this book.

Dr. Martha Garland, Vice Provost for Undergraduate Education at The Ohio State University, helped launch the final stages of the project. Readers Julie Stonefelt, Anne and Katie Chasser, Gay Hadley, Joann Bromberg, Susan Little, and Leigh Calvez gave me encouragement and good advice. My brother Tom Unkefer gave me new ways to think about the book. Janette Baugh provided a peaceful room for writing the manuscript. Joan Graham introduced me to a group of writers who sharpened my thinking. My agent Anne DePue and my attorney Sheila Clark served as superb advocates and representatives.

Finally, a big thank you to my husband, Weldon Ihrig, who supported this idea from the beginning and never doubted the outcome.

Introduction

EVEN THOUGH I am a Certified Public Accountant, financial planner, and a former university administrator, when I sent my son Alan off to college I gave him very little instruction about how to manage his money. I told him I would pay his tuition, and we negotiated a monthly allowance. It was his job to handle all the other expenses beyond tuition with the check I sent and the money he saved on his own. I thought it would be a good exercise for my son to manage a monthly stipend, but that was the extent of my training for him.

It didn't occur to me to tell him what to look for when he chose a bank, how to write a check, why he should balance his checking account, let alone show him how to prepare a budget for living expenses, explain how to make decisions on nonessential purchases like a car, or describe the need for renter's and health insurance.

I was sent to college with no financial instructions and I did alright. I thought my son would get along just fine, and he did—for a while. He did not have access to credit cards while he was a student. He did not have a personal computer, cell phone, or pager—expensive accoutrements considered necessary by most college students today. Even so, by the time Alan turned thirty, he declared bankruptcy because of overwhelming credit card debt. I was heartsick knowing I might have prevented his financial crisis by giving him a better foundation in money management while he was in high school and college. This book shows you how to avoid Alan's mistakes and learn to manage your finances.

Shortly after I moved to Seattle in 1996, I began consulting with a private student loan association. As I worked with the staff, they told me how worried they were that students with little experience in personal finance were able to borrow large amounts of money. They wanted to talk with a financial planner about the money management tools students need when they start their college careers. I learned that colleges and universities were also concerned about their students' money-handling issues—some were even hiring financial planners to help students.

The stories of students' problems reminded me of some of my middle-aged clients who still did not understand money basics and were struggling with their finances. They knew they needed to get on firmer financial ground, but it was hard for them. I found that many clients never learned basic skills about handling money: how to create a realistic spending plan, how to control credit card spending, how to determine a safe level of debt, and how to save. I even had clients who could not balance their checking account and never knew how much money they had in the bank. When they started bouncing checks, they simply opened another account and started fresh.

You are being asked to shoulder more financial responsibility than students in previous generations. There is no grace period for you; from the first day on campus, you are bombarded with major financial responsibilities, and the ways you decide to manage your money in college will probably be your money management pattern for the rest of your life. That is why it is so important to get firmly grounded in financial basics.

I thought if I could provide fundamental information about money management—information that does not appear in the multitude of financial-planning books on the market—then you would have a greater opportunity to begin your working life in a solid financial position.

In the following chapters, I tell stories of students who had lessons to learn about money when they went to college and the financial knowledge they wish they had mastered before leaving home.

These stories have been compiled from interviews I conducted with college students, recent college graduates, and college and university administrators around the United States. Many openly shared financial lessons they learned. I consolidated their most critical issues and distilled them into stories that I think you will find useful. After each story, I detail the information gleaned from the stories and suggest practical ways to begin setting up and maintaining a financial life.

My aim in writing this book is to help you operate from a position of self-knowledge and control, to reduce the unknown and anxiety-provoking aspects of money management, and to provide a solid financial basis on which to build the rest of your life in a secure and fulfilling way. My wish for you is that this knowledge will put you on the path to making *smart* financial decisions and to becoming the *master* of your financial life.

1

Seduced by Credit Cards

"WE CAN LOAN you enough money to get out of debt," a sign on a bank proclaims. Sometimes credit cards are viewed that way. Students look at easy access to credit as extra money, not a debt that will have to be repaid. When I asked Jason to tell me what he wished he had known about money when he went to college he said, "No question about that. In two words, credit cards."

JASON'S STORY

I was seduced by credit cards. I couldn't quit using them. I kept collecting more and more to feed my addiction. I charged meals, magazines, movies, and mochas. I got into heavy debt. I didn't know what was happening. I woke up and found I owed close to $4,000. And worst of all, I had nothing to show for all that debt.

I remember when I got my first credit card. *I was still in high school and I felt as though I'd arrived—I was finally an adult because I had a credit card. I took a lot of pride in being able to charge things, you know, at the mall, buying movie tickets, and at the music store. I enjoyed taking people out to eat and paying for the meal. Before I got the credit card, my* *friends and I always paid for our own food. After I got the card, I was the big shot and I loved picking up the tab.*

I had a job and always paid the monthly minimum amount on the credit card statement. I thought that was the correct way to handle my payments. Now I know the minimum amount was based on a ten-year repayment period and a hefty interest charge was added to my account every month I didn't pay off the balance. Imagine! I would be paying for those mochas long after I graduated from college.

I signed up for every credit card offer that arrived in the mail. By the time I went to the university, I had five credit cards in my wallet. I felt rich. I wasn't worried about having so many cards. After all, these companies asked me to take their cards, so I thought it was okay. I believed it would be good to establish a credit rating by having credit card debt. I figured the more I had, the better I looked.

I charged just about everything on my cards—from breakfast to concert tickets. I even charged my groceries. Then there were all the things I enjoyed—especially music. My CD collection grew and grew. And so did the balances on my credit cards.

Near the end of my first year of college *I started maxing out on most of my cards. It startled me. How could I have spent that much money? I didn't have much to show for it. I was still paying the minimum monthly payment on each card, but I couldn't charge any more. I considered getting another card so that I could keep spending. I felt like I was in this debt trap I didn't know how to get out of. I was scared I would add more debt if I got another credit card, and at the same time I wasn't sure if I could stop spending.*

I thought about talking to my parents, but I was afraid they'd be mad, and to be honest, I was embarrassed. Here I was, finance major headed for Wall Street and I couldn't control my own spending.

Then I got lucky. One afternoon at the student union, I ran into a guy from my dorm. Gabe came to college after doing a stint in the navy, so he was a little older than most of my friends and had more experience. We got to talking and I blurted out that I was worried about my credit cards.

Gabe said that he viewed credit cards as a convenience and a backstop for emergencies, but he never used them to finance day-to-day expenses. He said they were way too expensive for that. He illustrated his point by showing me a simplified example about how interest compounds.

If I bought a $20 pizza and financed it through my credit card at 20 percent interest, at the end of the first year that pizza would be $24 (20% of $20 or $4 interest plus $20). At the end of the second year, the cost would be $28.80 (20% of $24 or $4.80 interest plus $24). I saw that I was paying interest not only on the pizza but also on the previously charged interest. Making the monthly minimum payment would only put a small dent in the debt. But the credit card companies don't figure interest once a year, they add it every month or even daily so the debt is growing even faster than Gabe's simple example demonstrated.

This information blew me away. I could easily see how I might not ever get out of debt. It was scary and I had to make changes. Gabe suggested I make a list of all my credit cards, the amount I owed, the minimum monthly payment, the interest rate, and the annual fee. I didn't even know I was paying an annual fee on a credit card. It turned out I was paying a fee for the two cards I had—a fee for the opportunity to build up debt!

Credit Card Debt

CREDIT CARD	TOTAL OWED	MONTHLY PAYMENT	INTEREST RATE	ANNUAL FEE
1.	$ 750.00	$ 20.00	15%	$ 60.00
2.	869.00	22.00	18%	35.00
3.	425.00	10.00	22%	
4.	956.00	30.00	15%	
5.	667.00	20.00	19%	
Total	$ 3,667.00	$ 102.00		$ 95.00

Gabe told me not to use the credit cards anymore—to cut them up and go on a strictly cash basis. He said I could always use a bank debit card in situations where I ordinarily use a credit card. The beauty of a debit card is that it has the convenience of a credit card and the amount I spend is automatically deducted from my checking account.

We looked at the list of what I owed. Gabe told me I needed to start paying down the balances. He said to pay as much as I could each month to the credit card charging the highest interest rate, while continuing to pay the minimum amount on the other cards.

I rethought about talking with my parents. *Gabe said his parents had helped him with a financial problem when he first set out on his own, and he encouraged me to ask for my parents' advice. I was going home in a few weeks. I decided to swallow my pride and talk with Dad.*

My dad was working on his income taxes when I got home. He said he needed a break and asked me to go for a walk with him. It seemed like a good time to tell him about my credit card problems.

The numbers, both the amount I owed and the number of credit cards I had, shocked him. In fact, he told me he didn't realize that a college student could get credit cards. He wasn't able to get a credit card until he'd graduated from college and had a full-time job.

Dad was really happy I was paying my bills on time. He said I was building a credit history and when you're first starting out, it's a good idea to establish a credit rating by having a little debt to demonstrate that you will be responsible for paying it off. But in my case, it was more important to conquer my credit card spending than to worry about a credit rating.

Even dad had to be careful about using his credit cards. *He said it's so easy to use them and not think through the purchase. He told me he had to find ways to protect himself from getting into credit card debt. Now he only had two cards—one for business travel and one for emergencies—and he only used them for those purposes.*

I was so relieved after my dad told me about his difficulties with credit cards. Then I told him about Gabe and our conversations about money. Dad looked impressed, especially when I told him how I had quit using my credit cards. I asked him to help me figure out my options for getting my debt paid off.

We brainstormed and made a list of options:

- Leave school for one term to make enough money to pay off the cards.

- Reduce my spending on extras like eating out, CDs, and expensive entertainment.
- Give up my cell phone.
- Live at home to decrease expenses and attend community college until the debt is paid off.
- Lengthen the time I take to pay off the cards. Instead of shooting for one year, as Gabe suggested, try to graduate from college with no credit-card debt. In other words, take three years to pay them off rather than one.
- Get a part-time job during the school year and apply the earnings to my debt.

We discussed the pros and cons of each option:

- I didn't want to interrupt my education. I needed to finish college in four years and get on with my life.
- It was essential to reduce my spending. Things had gotten out of hand since I started using credit cards, and I knew I was reckless about my spending.
- I decided not to cancel my cell phone. It was important to me, and I thought I could more easily save on other expenses.
- I was happy at my college. I didn't want to give up the life I established and the friends I made. Moving home would make me feel like I had failed. Moving home was a last resort.

The last two options had possibilities. I had three years until graduation, and I was paying $102 per month on my debt. If I didn't use the cards and continued paying, I would be close to being debt-free by graduation. If I combined that approach with earning extra money during the school year, I could definitely be out of debt by graduation. So that's what I decided to do—earn extra money at a part-time job during the school year and set a goal of being free of expensive credit card debt in three years.

I looked for ways to cut my spending. *I started using the public library for magazines and leisure reading. I used to buy books and magazines, but when I considered the amount of money I sank into this, I* *realized that small change adds up fast.*

Music is important to me, and I found shops that sold used CDs. I was amazed at how quickly new releases would show up in these stores, and if I was tempted to buy a new CD (and I was tempted) I would remind myself of my goal. It worked.

I was cautious about eating out. I still enjoyed sharing a meal and conversation with friends, but I selected less expensive meals to keep the cost down and limited the number of times I went out to eat.

I discovered that I could tolerate reading used textbooks. I shopped early to find books in the best possible condition and lowered my book budget.

I examined the entertainment options offered on campus. Often, discounted tickets for students were available, and my friends and I had some great times by taking advantage of free entertainment on campus.

The good news *is that I paid off the cards early. It took about two years, and by the time I was a senior I had no debt. That was a great day for me.*

My attention to my finances also influenced my career decision. During my second year in college, I started thinking about a career in education rather than finance. I understood I would never make a huge salary in teaching, but now I knew I could manage on a teacher's pay. I had my spending under control. A huge weight had been lifted. I felt calmer and steady. I didn't need to buy things to get a lift.

CREDIT CARD EXPLOSION

Credit card debt among students is growing by leaps and bounds. A survey by Sallie Mae, a major student loan provider, showed that 78 percent of undergraduates have an average of three credit cards, and 32 percent have four or more cards. The average student credit card balance in 2000 was $2,748, up from $1,980 in 1998, and more than double the average from 1993. The survey also found that one in ten will graduate with balances exceeding $7,000.

As I interviewed students and administrators about financial issues, I heard many stories of the difficulties students were having with credit cards. When I asked them to speculate about why credit-card debt was increasing so rapidly, they pointed to the expensive lifestyles many students try to sustain. They told me some parents wanted their children to maintain the same level of abundance in college as they had at home. Perhaps this comes out of the affluent period of the 1990s, when we thought the economy would stay strong and many saw an unexpected increase in personal net worth due to the rising stock markets. Many people began to feel rich and spent as though they were, but the new millennium brought a different economy, with huge losses in personal wealth and a deep-rooted concern about the economic future. It's time to review our attitudes concerning money and look again at financial basics.

Jason was lucky and wise. He stemmed the debt he was unknowingly building and was able to work out a reasonable way to get out of debt and learn to live within his resources.

FINDING YOUR WAY

For many of you, learning to manage credit cards will be your first money-handling challenge. Credit cards are ubiquitous. Credit cards do not seem like real money. Credit cards lead to real debt. There is little awareness when using the card that the bill still has to be paid. And often when the monthly statement comes in, the balance is startling. You wonder how on earth you managed to charge that much!

Then the ostrich effect sets in. It is so easy to ignore your debt level, to push it out of your mind and continue using the credit card indiscriminately. It is tempting to say one day I will be earning more money and *then* I will pay off my debt. *Then* never comes.

The reality is credit cards are convenient and useful, but they are terribly seductive. As a new user of credit, you will want to ensure that you are ready to manage credit cards before you get into debt.

TECHNIQUES FOR MANAGING A CREDIT CARD

One of the best ways to begin to test your ability to use a credit card responsibly is to get a card with a low credit limit—around $200 to $500. Refuse offers from the credit card companies to raise your credit limit. Make the commitment to pay the card off every month. Promise yourself that if you cannot pay the entire balance, you will not use the card until you have saved enough money to cover the outstanding balance. With the protection of a low credit limit, if your spending does get out of hand and you cannot pay off the balance, you will not have a huge debt because of the low limit on your card.

Study your behavior using a credit card versus using cash. Does your decision making change when you use the card? Are you having difficulty viewing the card charges as real money? Do you buy things with credit cards that you would not buy if you were operating on a cash basis?

Determine the monthly amount of money you can afford to charge on your credit card. Then access your account online daily or weekly to review how much you have charged. Monitoring the balance will help you control spending when you view what you have already charged.

Consider giving yourself a weekly charging limit. Examine your credit card balance online every morning. If you approach your weekly limit, stop spending until the following week. You will gain a feeling of control and the knowledge of your credit card balance will ease your worries about overcharging.

FREEZE YOUR CREDIT CARD

A Ph.D. in economics who lectures graduate students about money management told me about an interesting method to contain credit card usage. He advises students to freeze their credit cards in a big bowl of water when they believe they may be tempted beyond their means. This technique buys time—time to consider a purchase and decide if it is affordable and truly desired.

He decided to test his method personally, since he recognized that he often spent indiscriminately, especially on weekends. He froze his credit cards in a bowl of water on a Friday night. Saturday he went out shopping and found an appealing water fountain for his office. He thought it would bring a soothing sound to his work environment. But he couldn't buy it—not enough cash.

When he got home, his wife found him in the kitchen with the frozen credit cards. He was trying to decide whether he could microwave them or use hot water to melt the ice.

When he told his wife why he needed the credit card, she said, "But sweetheart, we already have a fountain. Dad gave you one for your birthday. It's in the hall closet."

OTHER CREDIT CARD MANAGEMENT TECHNIQUES

Another way to curb the impulse to use credit cards is to put a small sticker on the card—maybe a red dot or a picture of your favorite cartoon character. When you see that image on the card as you use it, stop and ask yourself if you can afford to pay for the item when the bill comes. If you know you won't have the money, remember that your $20 pizza will end up costing $40 if you only make the minimum monthly payment. Ask yourself if you still want to be paying for that pizza in ten years.

Often, a credit card company will generously offer to increase your line of credit. You don't have to accept their offer. If you are satisfied with your limit, write or call the company and tell them you do not want your credit line increased. Later on, if you find you need a higher limit, you can request an increase.

If you find you are not able to control yourself using a credit card, switch to your bank check card or debit card. Cut up the credit card, get the balance paid off, and cancel the card. The check or debit card gives you most of the ease of paying as a credit card. The critical part is making sure you enter your purchases in your check register so that you do not overdraw your checking account. When you feel ready to try credit cards again, you will have no problem getting one.

If you get home after a shopping trip and realize that you have spent beyond your means, return your purchases. Most stores cheerfully credit your account if the price tags are intact and you have your receipt. Or, have the store hold an item you are interested in purchasing for twenty-four hours. This will give you time to coolly reassess your ability to pay and whether you really want or need the item. Remember the water fountain.

Have a ready response for new credit card offers. As you walk by the table at the student union offering incentives to sign up or you get a telephone offer, just say, "No thanks. I only need one."

Always be aware of the cost of your credit cards. If you carry debt, be sure to use the card with the lowest interest rate. But always aim for being free of credit card debt.

Study the steps Jason used to clear his debt. He defined his problem by writing down all the information about his debt. Then he listed all the remedies that would help him reduce his balances. He acknowledged that he had to get rid of his credit cards. He did not trust himself to be disciplined about not using them, so he cut them up. This was hard for him—it is hard for most people to destroy their cards. If he had not been able to abolish them, he could have asked his dad or a trusted friend to hold the cards for him—someone who would question why he wanted to use the cards if he felt the desire.

After Jason made the commitment to getting out of debt, he approached the problem logically. He chose the card with the highest interest rate and made bigger payments on that card until it was paid off. Then he picked the next most expensive card.

Keep your future in mind. Envision yourself graduating from college and starting a new career. Imagine the freedom you will experience starting your professional life without the oppression of expensive debt. You will be able to live a better life.

It is easier to control spending in college than it ever will be later on. After all, students are not expected to have much money and if you can manage your debt, you will have more a prosperous life after graduation.

SPECIFIC GUIDELINES

Perhaps the easiest way to manage your credit card debt (if you carry a balance from month to month) is to listen to the advice of Dr. Lucia Dunn, Professor of Economics at The Ohio State University, a researcher of credit card behavior. According to Dunn, "Our research shows that the following situations put a card user in a high-risk category for default, with all the adverse consequences that this will entail:

If the card user is carrying an unpaid balance greater than one-third of their total credit limit from all cards.

If the total minimum monthly payment (from all cards) that a card user owes amounts to 5.5% or more of their total monthly income.

These are the danger zones that should alert a credit card user to the fact that they may have used their cards excessively and that they may need to rein in their charging behavior to avoid default."

Default means failing to make a minimum monthly payment on time. Dunn also notes that the more credit cards one has, the more likely one will default on payments.

Jason had a total credit limit of $4,000 on his five cards. Using Dunn's suggestion, he should never have an unpaid balance of more than $1,320 carried from one month to the next ($4,000 x .33). But Jason had almost maxed out his five credit cards and owed $3,667—almost triple the guidelines. If Jason limited his credit cards to one with a credit line of $1,000 he would have been safer from accumulating overwhelming debt.

ESTABLISHING A CREDIT HISTORY

A good credit rating is important, and the first way to establish your history is to pay your bills on time. Having debt and demonstrating that you are responsible in making regular payments will also add to your credit report, but do not take on debt for this reason until you are confident in your ability to make the monthly payments. Having numerous credit cards will not enhance your credit history, in fact, lenders look at credit cards as debt, even if there is no balance owed. So if you have a lot of credit cards, you could be turned down for additional loans because it appears to the creditors that you are burdened with debt. Jason's dad said it best: at this point in your life it is more important to learn to manage credit cards than to enhance your credit history.

You can view your credit history as important as your academic transcript. Some top medical schools now require that admitted students stay out a year to get their finances in order if they have a poor credit rating and/or are carrying excessive credit card debt. The reason is simple. Graduate and professional school administrators know one of the biggest reasons for student dropout is financial. These schools don't want to admit a student only to have him leave at the beginning of the second or third year. It leaves an opening the school cannot fill.

ASK FOR HELP

Another danger with using credit cards is that people may get into so much debt that they feel the situation is hopeless—they believe they will never be able to pay off the balance. Some of you will build up large debt using your credit cards or you may already have debt that you feel is oppressive. What should you do if you find yourself in this situation? The first thing you should do is to seek help. Look for resources on campus that will help you work through solutions.

Go to the student financial aid office, even if you have not had contact with them before. Ask to see a counselor who can help you with your credit card issues. Financial aid officers are concerned about mounting credit card debt, and most offices have staff trained to help with financial problems or who can direct you to a helpful source.

If you are depressed go to the student health services and ask to see a counselor. There have been suicides reported among a few college students who were so weighted down with debt that they took their own life. But a person does not need to be suicidal to benefit from professional counseling. Talking with another person, laying out the problems and getting reactions and ideas often help a person work through issues more quickly.

Almost every community has a Consumer Credit Counseling office that provides advice, classes, and help for people to work out reasonable plans to reduce their debt and to learn to manage their resources. It is a free service and many people have worked their way out of debt with the help of Consumer Credit Counseling.

Most financial-planning books advise you to be disciplined about using your credit cards. This is good advice, but it does not work for everyone. Some people need more assistance in managing their spending habits, particularly credit cards, than others, and if you are one of those people, don't be shy or embarrassed about asking for help. Many university administrators expressed their concern about students' finances and their desire to aid them in becoming better money managers. We all have to learn about money handling, and using available resources that work for you is smart and responsible.

CREDIT CARDS ARE USEFUL

There are good reasons for having a credit card:

- For emergencies.
- To rent a car.
- To provide a concise record of spending.
- To dispute a charge. Since you have not yet paid for the item it is easier to have the credit card company question the charge than if you paid cash.
- To build a good credit history.

Credit cards are a useful financial invention. They have changed our economy, made life simpler, and challenged us, the users, to more sophisticated money management behavior.

Our job as consumers is to find our own best way to manage credit, to be fully informed about the cost of using a credit card and the cost of carrying debt on it, and to understand our unique reaction to the availability of credit cards.

FINANCIAL BASICS

- When getting your first credit card, request a low credit limit until you know what you can manage.

- Don't fall in the trap of accumulating many credit cards. You only need one credit card.
- If you can't control your credit card spending, cut up the card or freeze it in a bowl of water.
- If you carry debt on your credit card, do not let the amount carried from one month to the next exceed one-third of your credit limit.
- Don't be afraid to ask questions. Ask family and friends to share financial tips, and if you need professional help seek out a counselor at your school's health center or contact the Consumer Credit Counseling office in your community.

2

Nervous Breakdown Budget

JODI LEFT FOR college with personal accounting software and a detailed budget. Jodi was intent on keeping track of her spending and in the process discovered some important clues to her financial nature.

JODI'S STORY

My budget drove me crazy. I never dreamed I would get so upset over keeping track of my money. I was confident about my finances when I left for college. I had a budget with categories for every expense I could think of like laundry, dry cleaning, shoe repair—lots of detail so that I would know exactly where every cent was spent. But I couldn't keep up with my plan. It got to the point my hands shook when I sat down to pay my bills or look at my accounts. I finally realized I was being burdened by a budget and accounting system that was too detailed and extensive for me to live with.

Mom helped me develop a budget for college. *We discussed how we would pay for college. I would take out a student loan for part of the*

Jodi's Budget

EDUCATIONAL COSTS	Month	Term	Year
Tuition		$ 4,000	$ 8,000
Textbooks		600	1,200
Computer		100	200
Supplies		80	160
Room & Board		3,000	6,000
Total		$ 7,780	$ 15,560

LIVING EXPENSES

	Month	Term	Year
FOOD			
Groceries	10		90
Restaurants	50		450
Snacks	25		225
Coffee	40		360
TRANSPORTATION			
Bus	10		90
Trips home	20		180
CLOTHING			
Purchases	25		225
Laundry	5		45
Dry cleaning	10		90
Shoe repair	2		18
INSURANCE			
Personal property	10		90
ENTERTAINMENT			
CDs	20		180
Concerts	25		225
Movies	30		270
Plays	25		225
Books	20		180
Magazines	10		90
Vacations	30		270

(continued next page)

Jodi's Budget (cont.'d)

	Month	Term	Year
PERSONAL GROOMING			
Haircuts	25		225
Shampoo, hair products	5		45
Makeup	8		72
Feminine Needs	6		54
Deodorant	2		18
Perfume	5		45
Soap	2		18
Other	5		45
MISCELLANEOUS			
Gifts	15		135
Charitable	15		135
Cell phone	35		315
Yoga classes	20		180
Photography club	15		135
Cushion	53		477
TOTAL	$ 578		$ 20,762

tuition and would be responsible for my personal expenses. Mom would pay the rest of my tuition, room and board, and books.

We requested a booklet from my future college that outlined the costs a typical college student could expect. We studied the booklet and discussed what I would need. I quizzed my older sister Sophie about her experiences with college costs and talked with a girlfriend of Sophie's who went to the same school I planned to attend.

I purposely made my budget a generous one, just to be sure I would have enough money. Mom said I could adjust the plan after I had some experience and was sure of my costs. She showed me how to use an accounting software program so I could track all my expenses against the budget we created.

Once I got to college, I paid my bills twice a month and entered all the *data into the computer. I felt that I had to keep track of every cent or the program wouldn't balance, so I carried a little notebook with me to jot down every cash expense. This wasn't easy for me. The level of detail wore me out. I got so tired of trying to keep track of every little cent. Finally, I couldn't deal with it anymore and I quit trying.*

***Unfortunately, I went from one extreme to the other.** I abandoned tracking my finances and spent what I wanted. I signed up for a credit card thinking the monthly bill would provide me with information about how I was spending my money. And I made sure to pay the balance off every month, to avoid paying those high interest rates.*

I continued to pay my bills twice a month, but quit paying attention to my expenses. I didn't bother to balance my bank account; I didn't even keep a running total of the cash balance in my checkbook. I had plenty of money in my account because I had deposited all my savings into my checking account, so I wasn't worried about bouncing checks. I was burnt out with finances.

When I returned home for the summer, my mom said it was time to review my past year's finances. She didn't know I had quit following the plan we had set up and had not balanced my bank account for six months. I finally told Mom what had happened. She looked surprised and asked me why. When I explained how budget tracking was so exhausting I couldn't face doing it anymore, she nodded her head in understanding.

***Mom apologized.** Can you believe it? She said leaving home and taking on responsibility for my own financial life was a big step, and she didn't realize that I would get so overwhelmed by the budget process she had laid out for me. She said I had to find my own way around handling money. I had to look for those special techniques that work best for me.*

She thought my money breakdown came from my math background; I thought my finances could be translated into strict mathematical laws, and when there were deviations it threw me. She asked me to start thinking about what upset me around money.

***I returned to my budget** and looked at what I had spent during the time I had been accounting for every penny. I printed out my expenses for the first three months at college. I pulled out all the predictable things—items* *that didn't deviate much from month to month like bus fare, cell phone, and monthly photography club dues. Then I looked at the other items—the ones that really gave me fits when I tried to stick to a budget: eating out, snacks, coffee, magazines, and entertainment.*

I studied my numbers, looked at my credit card statements and saw some patterns. When I dumped my accounting system and started using the credit card, the "little things" doubled. I was spending about $75 a week when using cash, but when I went to a credit card and quit tracking my expenditures, I spent closer to $125. Amazing. I had no idea. I was sure I could keep my cash needs to $75 a week if I paid attention.

This is what I decided to do: *every Monday I withdrew $75—my allotment for the week—from the bank. This was for all the day-to-day expenses like snacks, coffee, magazines, movies, and other small items. Every morning I counted the amount of money left in my wallet. I thought about the rest of the week and what I would be doing that would cost money. That way, if I knew something more expensive was coming up on the weekend, I would be careful during the week by not overindulging on snacks or magazines or books.*

If I had money left over at the end of the week, I locked it in my desk and used it in those weeks when I overspent my allotment. Some weeks I had a lot left over. Other weeks I ran short by the middle of the week and pulled some of the extra cash from my desk. It all seemed to even out over the semester.

I created a simpler, less detailed budget. *It was easier to keep track of my spending because, other than my weekly cash allowance, I always paid with a check or credit card. I wanted to monitor what I was spending so that I didn't fall short of funds later in my college career.*

This system was successful, *and I was relieved to have a routine that made me feel in control without all the anxiety. Of course, the key to this method was I had tracked my expenditures carefully during the first three months at college, so I had good information on my spending patterns, and I knew how much cash I typically spent during the week.*

Mom and I had a monthly telephone conversation about how I was doing with my money. It was reassuring to have someone to talk to, and

Jodi's Simplified Monthly Budget

Cash	$ 300
Cell phone	35
Clothing purchases	25
Concerts	25
Cushion/emergency fund	50
Gifts	15
Personal property insurance	10
Photography club	15
Plays	25
Trips home	20
Vacations	30
Yoga class	20
TOTAL	**$ 570**

knowing I would review my financial situation every month helped me stay on target.

I thought a lot about my money-handling lessons that summer. *For me, budgets are useful to try to get a fix on the total cost of living. But I learned that a budget doesn't work precisely as I thought it would. Little things pop up from time to time that simply can't be anticipated. A shower gift for a friend, paying for class handouts, computer repairs—you can't predict these things. Unexpected surprises threw me into a tizzy and made me throw up my hands in disgust about keeping a budget. But when I realized that the unexpected is normal, that's when I understood why a cushion is important.*

Every month I pay my bills, balance my checking account, and generally look over how I managed my money for the month. The key word here is generally. I got rid of the shaking hands and fear around money when I stopped being manic about each and every detail. I still paid attention. I knew my financial circumstances. I became responsible about money again. I just needed to find the right way for me to manage my situation.

PURPOSES OF A BUDGET

Constructing a budget for a brand-new lifestyle isn't always easy. Let's look at why you should make the effort:

- To know how much it will cost to go to college.
- To determine if you have enough money to go to the college of your choice.
- To plan how to get the money you will need or adjust your college selection.
- To give you pertinent information when making decisions on expenditures beyond normal, basic needs.

GETTING STARTED

Jodi and her mom had a good approach to developing a list of her expenses for college. They consulted a publication produced by her future college that showed the typical expenses for a college student at her school and in her college town. Those estimates are generic and often conservative, so Jodi further pursued information by talking with older college students to get their practical knowledge about college expenses.

It is always wise to add a little extra for expenses. It is almost impossible to create a precise budget—either while you are in college or when you begin your working life. Some expenses do not become apparent until you are on campus. This does not mean budgets are worthless. It means you create a plan, monitor your activity, then go back and adjust.

Sometimes people react to a strict budget the way many people handle diets. Everything is carefully noted and the plan is followed precisely for a few weeks. Then if there is one deviation from the plan, maybe a candy bar, the diet is discarded and the dieter feels that she has failed.

If your budget is too tight or unrealistic, you may feel like giving up when you don't follow it and then start spending more than you can afford. My suggestion is to either estimate your expenses slightly higher than you think they will be or build in a contingency amount—maybe 10 percent of your original plan—to cover those unexpected expenses. Then make the effort to track your expenditures carefully for two or three months. This will give you more information and you can adjust your plan accordingly.

Always give yourself some leeway in your financial planning. Remember Jodi's weekly cash allocation. Sometimes she didn't need all the cash, and other weeks she needed more than the weekly amount. If you build in a little extra to your spending plan, unexpected expenses will not discourage you.

A STEP-BY-STEP APPROACH TO ESTIMATING EXPENSES

- Gather information about the cost of attending the schools of your choice.
- Keep track of your spending for a month. This will give you good information on your daily spending pattern.
- Using a computer spreadsheet or a plain sheet of paper, write down all the expenses that the college lists.
- Adjust the college's suggested budget for anything you know will be different; for example, they show $1,000 for traveling home, but you live nearby and your cost will be minimal.
- Be sure to add a line for a cushion or unexpected expenses.
- Review your calculations with people who have some knowledge of college costs and/or keeping track of expenses, such as a parent, counselor, an older college student.
- Formalize your spending plan by copying it on a clean sheet of paper or set it up on your computer.
- Carefully track your spending for the first month of school. You don't have to account for every penny, but try to account for every dollar.
- At the end of the month, look at the results. Adjust the plan for your actual experience.

- Decide how you will keep track of your money in the future.

KEEPING TRACK

Once you feel confident in your money needs, you can decide how you want to manage your accounting.

Why you need to monitor your expenses:
- To determine if your original budget was correct.
- To adjust your budget for actual expenses after a few months of monitoring.
- To ensure that you are not spending beyond your means.
- For peace of mind.

Your behavior around monitoring your expenses is critical for you to observe as you begin taking on more financial responsibility. You need to find the most comfortable way to handle your money well, because this will probably be the way you manage your personal finances for the rest of your life.

MONEY MANAGEMENT OPTIONS

Some students use a spreadsheet program or personal accounting software and continue to account fairly closely for their expenditures. This is an excellent method and using a computer makes it so much easier. By tracking your expenses, you will quickly see if your budget is unrealistic or needs to be adjusted. If you begin to overspend, you will be able to study your spending data to see where the problem is. Some programs will allow you to import your checking account information online and balance your checkbook.

Other students get bogged down with so much accounting and have to find other methods to make sure they keep their spending in line. Jodi's method of using a fixed amount of cash every week to cover the day-to-day expenses is simple and effective. She simplified her spending plan so that she could easily track her spending and be sure to stay within her means. She paid for everything except her weekly cash allotment by check or credit card so that she had easy access to her information. And she thoughtfully reviewed her cash situation every day by counting her money and thinking about what the remaining cash would cover.

Jodi also saved time and money by getting cash once a week. The average college student uses her ATM card three times a week, and if she doesn't use an ATM provided by her bank she is paying a service charge—between $1.50 and $2.00 per transaction. If you work on a weekly cash plan, you will save time and money and will find it easier to maintain your spending plan.

Some people like to use the "envelope method" for keeping their spending in line. This is an old-fashioned system of putting cash for the week or the month in envelopes designated for a specific purpose such as groceries, entertainment, or gifts. When the money in the envelope is gone, they have to quit spending. While living in a group setting, it is important to keep the cash-filled envelopes locked up and secure. Even though this may be inconvenient, a number of people have had success with the envelope method, especially when operating on a careful spending plan.

Another way to manage your spending plan is to keep your money in a savings account and have the bank automatically transfer a specific amount of money into your checking account on a weekly or monthly basis. Jodi deposited all her money, $9,500, into her checking account, which allowed her to ignore how much she was spending. A better way to mange her money would be to put most of the $9,500 into savings. She would earn interest on the money and be forced to watch the cash in her checking account as she transferred money from savings to checking on a weekly or monthly basis.

Regularly transferring money when she needed it would give her an opportunity to think about her financial position and whether or not she was on track. She might not have spent $1,500 more than she planned during her first year of school if she had transferred the money into checking each month. Transferring funds between savings and checking accounts is also effective for those students who receive lump sums of money from grants and scholarships at the beginning of the term.

SPENDING PLANS

Because *budget* has a negative connotation, consider using the term *spending plan* to convey a forward-thinking, positive attitude about money, with a sense of control. The purpose of a spending plan is so that you will have an idea of what it will cost to live as you leave home and go to college. If you track your expenditures for a month or two, you will see if your original plan was reasonable or if you need to make adjustments. And, understanding your finances is the first step to mastering your money.

As you go through your college years, remember to consult your spending plan when contemplating new expenses. The director of financial aid at a small private university told me a good story to illustrate this point. He said the university had a few highly desirable apartments on campus. The right of first refusal went to student leaders. One spring, several students eagerly signed up for the following year. It was a prestigious address, but the students forgot that their housing cost would increase by $500 a month. The next fall, students visited the financial aid director complaining they lacked funds and requesting more aid. Fortunately, the director was able to help them, but he now makes sure that prospective renters take into account their higher cost of living before they request a more luxurious apartment.

MONITOR EXPENSES

Tracking your expenditures for a few months is critical. Not only will you be reassured about your finances, you will gain insights into your financial nature. You will begin to see where and when you tend to spend outside your plan. You can decide which types of expenditures are important to you and incorporate them in your budget. Or, you may decide that you can do without those purchases and work out a better way to control that type of spending. For example, Jodi found she purchased lunch every day at the local deli. She began to prepare sandwiches and eat with her friends in the courtyard. She not only saved money, but her circle of friends expanded.

LESSONS

I cannot tell you how many times I have heard middle-aged clients admit that they can't control their spending. More often than not, these clients were high wage earners who got into the habit of spending freely, without thought. They had huge mortgages, multiple car loans, and staggering credit card debt. They spent every cent they earned and more. They told me they felt out of control, they didn't know how to stop, and they were beginning to wonder if they could ever retire. Some of them described extreme reluctance and being fearful when it came time to pay their bills. One client was so unnerved by her money issues that she took tranquilizers before she came to see me to discuss her finances. It took a great deal of effort to work with these people to help them change their behavior and some of them never changed. They had instilled the habit of spending so deeply and for so long, they could not break the chains of debt.

My wealthiest middle-aged clients were steady spenders and savers. They didn't always make a huge salary but figured out ways to manage their money within their financial resources and personalities. They had little or no debt—certainly no credit card debt. They had savings, investments, and well-funded pension plans. They enjoyed life; they didn't pinch pennies; they had started early in their working years to live within their income and saved a portion of every paycheck.

START NOW

Your college years are a good time to identify and examine your financial predispositions, find the best ways for you to manage your money, and instill good money management practices in your daily life. That way, when you start to earn a regular paycheck you will be ready to take on bigger financial issues such as buying a car, saving for a home, supporting a family, and planning for retirement. You will feel steady and secure in your ability to plan for your financial future. Life will be easier knowing that you are in control of your financial life.

FINANCIAL BASICS

- Review your prospective college brochure for suggested student costs while attending their school.
- Ask a parent, family member, or an advisor to review your spending plan with you.
- Carefully track your spending for the first month of school, review and adjust your plan, then decide how you will monitor your spending in the future.
- Be mindful of expenses that are not important to you.
- Find your best way of allocating weekly cash amounts you need for expenses.

3

First in the Family

WITH ALL THE news stories about the high cost of a college education it would be easy for a person whose family did not have the resources or did not value higher education to plan to enter the workforce immediately after high school. That is what James planned until he discovered additional information about funding college.

JAMES'S STORY

How did I get to college? It was touch and go. There was no real encouragement from home. My parents hadn't gone to college, and I don't think it occurred to them that I should go. I naturally assumed I would follow my dad's path and work at the garage or learn to be a carpenter. That would have been a fine career for me, but I'm crazy about the work I do now as a mechanical engineer. Yes, I got an engineering degree, but I had a lot of help along the way.

Some of my high school teachers *started talking to me about my future. They were surprised to learn I didn't have any plans for further education. I think they assumed a good student would go on. When they learned I hadn't given it much thought and when I explained I couldn't* *afford to go, they encouraged me to explore my options for funding school.*

Mrs. Christensen, the senior counselor, took me under her wing that last year of high school. When I went in for the routine visit in the fall, she asked me about my plans for more education. I told her, frankly it would be nice to go to college, but I didn't see how I could manage it. My parents weren't in a position to help me financially, and I knew college was very expensive. On top of that, I didn't know what I would study if I did go.

Mrs. Christensen suggested something I found very unusual. She asked me to dream about what I would like to do if I could go to college. I think she wanted me to shift my thinking from a narrow outlook to surveying the possibilities. It was a wonderful lesson for me. I learned there are always ways of figuring out how to do something if it's important enough to me. I went back after a month of thinking about the future and told her my dream.

I knew I wanted to do something creative *and I enjoyed studying math and science. I met a mechanical engineer at my dad's garage, and as he described his work and what some of his associates had accomplished, I knew I could find satisfaction in that field.*

Mrs. Christensen encouraged me to start scouting out mechanical engineering programs. She had bulletins from various colleges in her office, and I found a lot of information on the Web.

I began to systematically look at the costs of going to school. I developed a worksheet so I could lay out the costs side by side. Then I looked at sources of funding—scholarships, grants, and of course, student loans. I was very nervous about borrowing money even though I knew it would be impossible to get through school without loans.

I began to ponder going to our community college *for one or two years so that I could live at home and save money. While I wanted to go away to college and have the full experience of living on a campus, my concern with money was more important. I opted to go to the community college for two years. I worked part-time; I got introduced to college life and gained more understanding of the finances of higher education. During those two years, I worked hard at my studies so my grades would be stellar. I hoped to receive more grant and scholarship money. After two years, my good record enabled me to transfer to the state university to enter their mechanical engineering program.*

I held off borrowing student loan money until the middle of my third year. My parents managed to give me a little money, and I lived carefully. I was intent on not borrowing any more than I absolutely had to. The costs at the state university were reasonable, and they had a good curriculum, but it was a five-year program and meant spending more money for an extra year. I landed good summer jobs, but even so, I graduated with close to $15,000 in student loans.

Having debt made me nervous, but I knew my starting salary would be at a level so I could repay the loans without too much trouble. In fact, I paid them off in two years by continuing to live like a student. Living a frugal life freed up money I would have spent on a nicer apartment and car. I knew if I increased my standard of living I wouldn't get out of debt for years, and I decided it was more important to get that part of my life under control so I could enjoy a better life later with no debt pressures.

It was the right way for me.

LOOK FOR ASSISTANCE

According to The Education Research Institute (TERI), one of the fastest-growing groups of student loan borrowers is from families where the student is the first in the family to go on to higher education. Often, the parents value higher education and offer a lot of moral support, even if they cannot provide the financial support. Other families do not know how to navigate the financial aid waters to gather the financial help needed.

It is up to you, the student, to seek out assistance. Tell your teachers and counselors that you want to go to college, but you do not know how to figure out how to get the resources to go. Ask them if they have any ideas. Do they have some firsthand experience with getting scholarships or grants? Do they know someone at a local college who would be willing to advise you? Ask for an introduction to this person and go see her.

Find older students in your community who have gone to college with initial limited resources. Talk with them about how they managed. Ask them to brainstorm with you on ways to come up with the needed money.

Start your quest for additional funds early. Begin gathering information eighteen months before you plan to start college. This will give you time to digest the information, fill out the required forms, and submit your requests before the deadline.

SYSTEMATICALLY DEVELOP INFORMATION

Here are some funding basics:

- Following the examples in chapter 2, list your costs of attending the schools that interest you. Write down your current sources of funds, no matter how small. This will tell you how much money you will have to find from other sources.
- There are three basic groups of additional funds:

    1. Scholarships
    2. Grants
    3. Loans

    Grants and scholarships do not have to be repaid. Loans must be repaid and almost always have interest charged on the unpaid balance.
- Start looking for scholarships immediately. Be cautious about paying for a service to find scholarships for you. You can do just as well using your computer to search for scholarships. Do not forget to look for scholarships given by organizations in your local community. Ask a guidance counselor if he has a list of all the local scholarships available. If you know where you will apply to college, contact their financial aid and scholarship offices and ask for help. Most colleges and universities have extensive Web sites that contain useful information. Check out http://www.college-scholarships.com, and http://www. finaid.org.
- Become an expert in the financing of your higher education. Go to the library for books on financial aid. Watch for newly published books that may not be in your

library yet and ask the librarian to order them for you. Search the Web for information pertaining to your specific interest of school and choice of study you wish to pursue. Talk with as many people as possible. Word of mouth often opens new doors and opportunities.

- The major need-based grants are:

  1. Federal Pell Grants
  2. Federal Supplementary Education Opportunities Grants (SEOG)

  Need-based means these funds are awarded on the basis of how much money you need to go to the school of your choice after taking into consideration your parents' and your resources. While these traditional grants do not cover as much of the cost of tuition as they were originally intended, it is a potential source of funds for you. Check them out.

- Your state may have grants available or your state may have funds combined with the federal government. Ask your counselor about availability in your state.

- Your college will probably have a work-study program. Federal money is provided to pay salaries for students to work on campus. The jobs are usually need-based, so talk with the financial aid office about availability.

- Next come the loan packages. This is funding which will have to be repaid, with interest. Take heart—70 percent of today's students have loans. The challenge is to borrow only enough money to get your degree. Investigate these federal loans first:

  1. Perkins
  2. Subsidized Stafford

  These federal loans are need-based, carry low interest rates, and the interest does not start to accrue until you graduate.

If you do not qualify or need more money, check into Unsubsidized Stafford loans. The federal government does not pay the interest on unsubsidized loans while you are in school. Interest starts accruing immediately and adds to the balance you will be required to pay back. Finally, there are numerous private sources. If you go to these alternative loans, shop around for the best terms. Compare fees, interest rates, and repayment terms before deciding.

If your parents are willing to borrow, PLUS loans may be available to them. Parents need to be totally aware of the cost and repayment schedule. For example, Parent Loan for Undergraduate Students requires payments and interest to begin about ninety days after the first check is issued. The interest rate tends to be about the same as a second mortgage. If your parents decide to borrow money for your education, make sure they take into account the money needed for four years of college, not just one year. Each year they will take on a new loan and additional payments.

LOOK FOR FUNDING OPTIONS

It may be that you cannot raise enough money to go to the college of your choice. Look for options to keep your costs down. James elected to live at home, attend a community college for two years, work, and save money so he could enroll at a public university for his last three years of school. If you plan to attend a community college and later transfer, check the requirements for transfer. Some public institutions are no longer automatically accepting students from community colleges. Budget constraints and highly qualified applicants are responsible for tightening acceptance of transfer students. Be sure you understand the rules so you can qualify for admission and have all your credits transfer.

Can you qualify for one of the military academies or for an ROTC scholarship? Some military scholarships provide funds for the entire program plus a monthly stipend for living expenses, in return for service in the military after graduation.

Does your academic major have cooperative programs where you can work in your field for one term, then attend classes for two terms? Engineering programs often offer this option. Ask your academic advisor for funding alternatives that pertain to your field.

Your only option may be that you have to go to school part-time and work in order to get your degree. Many people have done that. It is almost always best to get your degree as quickly as possible because you will earn a higher income once you finish school. But if speed is not an option for you, push on. Academic advisors suggest three hours of study for every hour in class for a B average. Use this guideline to calculate how many hours you can successfully spend on coursework. If you want your degree badly enough, you will succeed.

There are a number of examples in my family of people who could not get their degree in the traditional four years. One family member worked full-time at a public university and took advantage of their tuition reimbursement policy for pursuing a degree. She took two courses every quarter and got her degree in eight years.

I did not get my undergraduate degree until I was twenty-nine and a mother of two children. My graduation pictures show an exhausted young woman. It was hard, but I never regretted the effort I invested in my education.

KEEP YOUR CHIN UP

Ask experienced people for help and ask plenty of questions so that you fully understand your options. If you get discouraging advice, listen, take it under advisement, and double-check with other people to be sure it is accurate information. If you are given information you don't understand, find another person to explain the details. I tell my clients that if a financial professional, whether an insurance salesperson, stockbroker, or banker, cannot explain their products so the client understands what he is buying, then find someone else to deal with. In my experience, a person who cannot adequately explain a product or service may not entirely understand what he is talking about. The same advice holds for financial aid officers and other counselors you consult. You deserve full, understandable answers.

Some of the students I talked with said occasionally they were made to feel as though they were on the dole—using public funds as if they were on welfare. It was a negative experience and terribly unfair. Borrowing student loan funds is not being on charitable assistance—it is not a free handout. Receiving financial aid is taking advantage of a program that aids citizens to become better educated, which results in a benefit to society.

If you come across negative people, remember they are there to serve you. Also know that many college and university administrators are overworked and under pressure. Perhaps gentle persistence on your part will overcome their attitude. If not, look for another person to work with. Having worked in higher education for a number of years, I know how dedicated most of the staff are and how helpful they can be. Search them out.

TAKE RESPONSIBILITY

Filling out the forms required for applying for financial aid is not fun and it does take time, but there is a payoff for you, so put the effort into getting the forms completed and submitted before the deadline. One student I interviewed keeps a list of important deadlines in his organizer and always follows up with the appropriate office about a week after he submits his paperwork to be sure everything is in order. He believes it is important to establish a good relationship with a financial aid counselor. That way, if he needs help or advice, he knows he will get personal attention.

If your economic situation worsens—for example, a parent loses a job—go back to your financial aid counselor to determine if that makes you eligible for additional aid. Get to know your financial aid counselor, and when she does a particularly good job for you, send her a thank-you note.

LOAN REPAYMENT

James was so nervous about having debt that he lived in a manner that enabled him to repay his student loans in two years. This was a good decision for him, but it doesn't apply to everyone. Your student loans usually carry low interest rates—lower than interest on a car loan or even a mortgage. If you know that you will have to borrow money to start your professional career, probably for a car, review your loan situation carefully. To eliminate your debt quickly, pay off the most expensive loan first, then accelerate payments on the less expensive debt. Read chapter 11 for additional financial help as you start your career.

Take heart when looking at your student loan debt. According to a 2002 Census Bureau report, college graduates will earn almost a million dollars more over their lifetime than high-school graduates. While it is important to borrow no more than you absolutely need, the cost of your education may be the best investment of your life.

FINANCIAL BASICS

- Research all potential sources for funding your higher education: scholarships, grants, financial aid offices, books, and Web sites. The more you investigate, the more options you will find.
- Start your search for funds eighteen months before you plan to attend college.
- Ask experienced people for their advice and ideas in funding your higher education.
- Explore the less expensive route of attending community college for the first two years.

4

The Simple Things in Life

There are certain elementary facts of life to be learned about finances. When Jane went to college, she had no idea of the basics. Her parents always worked on a cash system, using money orders if they had to send money somewhere. She had to learn the basics from other sources.

JANE'S STORY

I got a big surprise when I arrived on campus. I knew financial aid and scholarships covered all my expenses, but I didn't expect to actually receive money. My parents rarely had extra money, didn't use banks, and always worked with cash on a week-to-week basis, so I was completely clueless (and ecstatic) when I got a big check for my living expenses at the beginning of the quarter.

My roommate said I'd better get that check in the bank *before I lost it. I told her I didn't have a bank—that I didn't know how to open a bank account or what to do once I had one. She suggested I call the financial aid office for advice. They responded by sending a list of all the banks in the campus area. This was helpful, but I still felt shy about walking into one of these places.*

I called my academic counselor and told him about my problem. Tom understood, asked me to stop by his office, and gave me a booklet his bank provided about the basics of checking. He went a step further. He pulled out his own checkbook and explained the purpose of a checking account. I began to understand that the bank provided a safe way to pay bills and keep money.

Tom showed me the checks and explained *how to fill one out properly. He said the check took the place of cash. He told me to be prepared to have identification handy when I wrote a check for merchandise, like buying books. Tom explained that I had to keep track of the checks I wrote by filling out the check register. And he showed me how I could keep track of how much money I had by subtracting the amount of the checks I wrote from the balance and adding any money I put into the bank. Tom assured me my money was safe—actually a lot safer than if I kept the cash in my room. He cautioned me not to spend all my money. It had to last for the entire term.*

Tom told me to come back when I got my first bank statement and he would teach me how to balance my account to make sure I knew how much money I had. A few months later Tom introduced me to an ATM card so that I could withdraw cash more conveniently.

What a relief *it was to get that money in the bank. I still felt a little nervous about not having the cash, but as I learned to use my checking account, I grew more confident and learned how to transfer money from checking to savings to earn interest. I was fortunate to have someone like Tom to show me how personal banking works.*

BASICS FOR EVERYONE

Most students come to college with checking account experience, but there is more to managing money than knowing how to write a check. Banking and managing personal accounts can be complex; banks are creating new products and charging more fees for services that used to be free. Living in a dormitory or apartment means that you must be more careful about securing personal documents.

As you read through this section you will find new information that will help you become a better money manager.

Opening a Checking Account

You probably only need a basic checking account. Here are some things you should know before you sign up for your account. The bank literature will provide you this information, or you can work through the questions with a banking person who should be able to answer your questions.

- What kinds of fees does the bank charge? Some examples of bank fees are: monthly service fees, charges for blank checks, per-check charges for writing more than a certain number of checks each month, and fees for returned checks.
- Where are their ATMs (automatic teller machines) located? If you go to an ATM not run by your bank, you will probably be charged a fee for using it. Try to avoid paying ATM fees by using your bank's machines.
- Does the bank have an online system you can use to review your account? This is a useful feature and will help you stay on top of your checkbook accounting. Is there a charge for using this system?
- Does your bank have a branch in your hometown and in your college town? If not, how will you manage the account when you're not in town?
- Does the bank offer overdraft protection? If you write a check for more money than you have in your account, will the bank cover the check using a line of credit similar to a credit card? You have to repay the money, but your check will not be returned to the payee. Some banks are now charging a fee every time the credit line is used. Be sure you understand how overdraft protection works, how you will be notified if you use it, and how to pay any charges made against the overdraft account.
- Does the bank offer a debit or check card?

- Does the bank offer a credit card? One way to begin building a credit history is with a low-limit credit card that you pay off every month. Remember, establishing a relationship with a bank will give you access to more services later on when you enter the workforce.
- Ask the bank to start your check number sequence on your blank checks at a number greater than 1 or 100. Start the numbering at 300, for example. A low-numbered check sometimes makes retailers nervous in accepting a check because the low number indicates a new account with no banking history.
- Consider ordering duplicate checks: checks that have a second copy which stays in the checkbook so that you have a record of the written checks.

HOW TO WRITE A CHECK AND USE A CHECK REGISTER

- Always use checks in numerical sequence, starting with the lowest number.
- Write the check in permanent ink. Use a pen whose ink slightly "soaks" into the paper. That way, a check cannot be altered after you write it. If using duplicate checks, be sure to press firmly as you write the check so that the information is clearly transferred to your copy.
- Fill in all the blanks including:

1. the date (day, month, and year)
2. the name of the payee
3. the numeric dollar amount
4. the spelled-out amount on the next line
5. your signature

Be sure to sign your checks the same way you signed the signature card at the bank.

- Record the information in the check register that came with your blank checks:

    1. check number
    2. date
    3. name of the payee
    4. amount of the check

- This is the way you will keep track of the money in your account and reconcile the balance with the bank information.
- Never sign a blank check or allow someone else to fill in the amount or payee. They may make a mistake or decide to write in a higher amount than you agreed upon. If it is your signature on that check, the bank will honor it and you will have to pay.
- If you make a mistake when writing a check, the best thing to do is record the check number in your check register, write VOID beside it, tear up the check, and write a new check. If you can't write a new check, you can correct the error on the check and put your initials beside the corrected error.

HOW TO KEEP TRACK OF THE MONEY IN YOUR CHECKING ACCOUNT

- You will receive a check register with your blank checks. This is where you record all the checking account transactions.

RECORD ALL CHARGES OR CREDITS THAT AFFECT YOUR ACCOUNT

NUMBER	DATE	DESCRIPTION OF TRANSACTION	PAYMENT/DEBIT (-)	√ T	FEE (IF ANY) (-)	DEPOSIT/CREDIT (+)	BALANCE $ 198 45
305	9/10	Manton Bookstore	$44 39	$	$		154 06
	9/11	Cash - ATM withdraw	75 00				79 06
	9/15	Paycheck				148 54	227 60
306	9/17	Basic Phone Co.	32 45				195 15
	9/17	Check card - Coffee Haven	4 15				191 00
307	9/20	University Photographers	50 00				141 00
	9/22	Check Card - Dean's Dress	64 27				76 73
308	9/25	Tammy's Drugery	18 21				58 52
	9/26	Check from Mom				250 00	308 52
309	9/27	University Library	24 00				284 52
	9/30	Paycheck				148 54	443 06

- Always use your blank checks in consecutive order. This way you'll know if you've forgotten to record a check or if one of your blank checks has been stolen.
- When you write a check, record:

  1. check number
  2. date
  3. name of the person or organization to whom you wrote the check
  4. amount of the check
  5. the new balance by deducting the amount of the check

- Record all your ATM withdrawals and your check card or debit card purchases in your check register daily. Deduct them from your balance.
- Record any bank service charges in your check register. You will find these charges on your bank statement when you balance your bank account or in some cases, like a charge for insufficient funds, you will receive a notice in the mail. Deduct any bank charges from the account balance.
- Be sure to record the amount you use to open the account. Record deposits with the date in the appropriate column. Add these amounts to your balance.

HOW TO BALANCE YOUR CHECKING ACCOUNT IN TWENTY MINUTES

Using the format of the bank statement as a guide:

- Start checking off the items listed in the bank statement in your check register:

  1. deposits
  2. checks written
  3. automatic deposits and withdrawals
  4. ATM withdrawals
  5. debit card or bank card charges
  6. bank charges

		RECORD ALL CHARGES OR CREDITS THAT AFFECT YOUR ACCOUNT					BALANCE	
NUMBER	DATE	DESCRIPTION OF TRANSACTION	PAYMENT/DEBIT (-)	√ T	FEE (IF ANY) (-)	DEPOSIT/CREDIT (+)	$ 198	45
305	9/10	Manton Bookstore	$ 44 39	√	$		154	06
	9/11	Cash – ATM withdraw	75 00	√			79	06
	9/15	Paycheck		√		148 54	227	60
306	9/17	Basic Phone Co.	32 45	√			195	15
	9/17	Check Card–Coffee Haven	4 15	√			191	00
307	9/20	University Photographers	50 00	√			141	00
	9/22	Check Card–Bloom's Dress	64 27	√			76	73
308	9/25	Jammy's Grocery	18 21				58	52
	9/26	Check from Mom		√		250 00	308	52
309	9/29	University Library	24 00				284	52
	9/30	Paycheck				148 54	443	06 *
	9/30	Bank Charge	8 50	√				
	9/30	Correct Balance					424	56 **

REMEMBER TO RECORD AUTOMATIC PAYMENTS / DEPOSITS ON DATE AUTHORIZED.

* Addition error
** See Bank Reconcilation form

Unkefer Savings and Loan
Simpson, Ohio 22333

Bank Statement
September 1 to September 30

Lisa Huntsman
212 Worley Hall
Simpson, OH 22333

BALANCE

Balance on 9/1	198.45
Deposits and Other Additions	398.54
Checks Paid	126.84
Other Withdrawals and Fees	151.92
Balance on 9/30	318.23

DEPOSITS

9/15	148.54
9/26	250.00
Total Deposits for September	398.54

CHECKS PAID

Number	Date	Amount
305	9/13	44.39
306	9/21	32.45
307	9/29	50.00

OTHER WITHDRAWALS AND FEES

Date	Description	
9/11	ATM 2930 25th	75.00
9/18	Coffee Haven	4.15
9/23	Sloan's Dress Store	64.27
9/30	Bank Charge - checks	8.50

Bank Reconciliation Forms

CHECKS AND WITHDRAWALS OUTSTANDING
List all checks or withdrawals that are not shown on the bank statement

Date	Check No.	Amounts
9/25	308	18.21
9/29	309	24.00

Total   42.21   Put total on Line D below

DEPOSITS AND ADDITIONS OUTSTANDING

Date	Amounts
9/30	148.54

Total   148.54   Put total on Line B below

STATEMENT BALANCING

A. Ending Balance shown on Bank Statement	318.23
B. Deposits and Additions Outstanding	148.54
C. Add Lines A and B	466.77
D. Checks and Withdrawals Outstanding	42.21
E. Subtract Line D from line C.	424.56

    This is your correct checkbook balance

- If you forgot an entry, write it in the check register and mark it off. If you made a mistake in an entry, correct the amount and check it off.
- Write down the ending balance shown on the bank statement on a blank sheet of paper or on the template often provided in the bank statement.
- Add any deposits shown in your check register but not shown in the statement (this usually occurs near the cut-off date of the bank statement) to the ending balance.
- Subtract any checks that have not cleared the bank from the ending bank balance.
- Now you have your bank balance. Enter this amount in your check register.
- If you decide to balance your checkbook more often by using the online capabilities of your bank, follow the same procedure.

SECURITY ISSUES

You need to protect your financial information especially when living in a dormitory or apartment with people who come and go or friends of roommates whom you may not know:

- Always use your blank checks in numerical sequence. If you notice a missing check number, check your account online or call the bank to find out the amount and to whom the check was written. If you did not write the check, notify your bank. It is the bank's responsibility to honor your signature only on a check, but it is your responsibility to report the stolen check.
- Keep extra blank checks locked up.
- Do not leave confidential information lying around. Use a drawer that can be locked to store your bank statements, credit card numbers, PINs, blank checks, and credit cards.
- Keep a list of your credit cards and debit cards with the

account number and the number of the financial institution in a safe place. Do not keep this information with
the cards. Put this information in another location so that
if a card is lost or stolen, you can report it immediately.
In most cases the credit card companies assume financial
responsibility above $50 for the misuse of your card—if
you report the loss.

- Consider devising a PIN (personal identification number) that can be used with all your accounts. That way
you can memorize it and will not have to write it down.
A PIN is used to access accounts online or through an
ATM.
- If you have written a check for something that is defec-
tive or for services not received and you are worried that
the check will be cashed, you can stop payment on the
check you have written, provided it has not cleared. The
bank usually charges a fee for this service.
- Always use a postal box to mail your checks; do not
leave the envelopes in an unsecured area where they
could be stolen.

TIMING

Remember that it usually takes about three days for a check or
debit card transaction to show up on the bank records, so be very
careful about accepting the accuracy of the bank's balance. There
could be checks still in the pipeline that are not yet deducted
from the account. Students get into trouble by accessing their
bank balance either online, telephoning the bank, or through an
ATM and using that balance as the amount of available funds. If
you are unsure about how much money you have in checking,
access your account online and, using the transactions after your
last statement from the bank, balance your checkbook. If you
can't get the level of detail that you need online, ask the bank to
give you a printout with the transactions after the last bank statement.

LUMP SUM PAYMENTS

Jane had another issue to deal with that could pose problems for the novice money handler. She received enough money to last the entire quarter. She had to pay for books, incidentals, school supplies, handouts, and personal needs throughout the term with this money. Receiving money in a lump sum at the beginning of the term had posed problems for several students I interviewed.

There are several ways to handle lump sum payments. One is to deposit the full amount in checking, but in the check register column for noting the balance, only put in the amount to be spent for the week or month. When you balance the bank account, add back the funds you have set aside for future spending.

A better way to manage the extra funds is to set up a savings account with your bank and either ask them to transfer the funds to your checking on certain dates or transfer the money yourself. This method is less confusing, will reduce spending errors, and you will earn interest on the money in savings.

INSURANCE

Be sure you are covered by health insurance. If you have been insured by your parents' policy, have them double-check to be sure you will continue to be covered when you leave for college. If you do not have health insurance, sign up for student health insurance with your college or university.

If you are taking expensive equipment such as computers or sound equipment to college, consider taking out an insurance policy to cover the theft or damage of these items. Your parents' home insurance policy may cover these items, but check with the insurance agent. It might be more beneficial and cost effective to have a separate policy.

CONTRACTS

At some point in your college career, you may decide to move into an apartment or house with roommates. There are some basic ground rules to establish before you finalize your relocation.

- Make an agreement with your roommates on how expenses are to be shared. Put it in writing so there will be no misunderstandings later.
- Read the lease. Carefully review:

    1. the length of the lease
    2. the rent
    3. security deposit
    4. terms for refund
    5. maintenance responsibilities
    6. any additional fees such as late payment penalties
    7. whether you can sublet

- Never sign a lease or a contract by yourself. You could be held solely responsible for any unpaid bills. Be sure that all your roommates sign every agreement including agreements with utility and telephone companies.
- Make sure the rent is paid on time. If not, it could adversely affect your credit rating.
- Check into renter's insurance. Renter's insurance pays to replace the contents of your apartment or house if you lose them in a burglary, fire, earthquake, or some other disaster.

INCOME TAXES

If you receive a W-2 or 1099 form in January, you must file a tax return. It is not difficult. A one-page simplified form usually suffices. It is usually to your benefit to file early because you will probably receive a refund. You can file your taxes online, and if you're due a refund, the IRS can electronically transfer the funds to your checking account if you fill out a form giving the pertinent information. You will get the refund faster, often in two weeks.

LOANS

Shakespeare wrote, "Neither a borrower, nor a lender be." It is still good advice when thinking of friends and money. If you loan money to a friend, be prepared to lose the friend and the money. This is harsh, but the reality is that a loan changes the composition of the friendship. While you may have a good relationship with this person, there is no guarantee that the loan will be repaid. Conversely, borrowing money may put a strain on a friendship that will ultimately destroy the relationship. And if you are no longer friends, you may feel less compulsion to pay back the money.

Never co-sign a loan for another person unless you are willing and able to take over the payments in the event that the borrower defaults. This situation may arise when borrowing money for a car.

We all want to lend a hand to our friends when they are in difficulty, and I am not suggesting that you do not help them. Make your decision on whether you can afford to loan money if the other person does not hold up his end of the bargain.

SEEK OUT HELP

Do not be shy about asking for help if you do not have experience in handling money. Advisors are good sources for finding trustworthy information. Bankers are available to give help and assistance. Ask trusted adults for help. Read this book and others to round out your knowledge. Learning to manage your finances is part of your education—a critical aspect of living in an ever-evolving monetary world.

FINANCIAL BASICS

- Deposit large sums of money not needed immediately into a savings account; transfer funds to checking as needed.

- Take the time to balance your checking and savings accounts.
- Keep blank checks and confidential information locked in a desk or file.
- If you are renting an apartment or house, be sure all your roommates sign the lease and utility agreements and look into renter's insurance.

5

Spend, Spend, Spend

SOMETIMES, WHEN sudden access to money is provided, a person cannot help spending it. Sometimes, especially when inexperienced in financial matters, the ability to live well is compelling. This is a cautionary tale about spending beyond one's means.

LESLEY'S STORY

I'm an accountant, so I should be an expert on financial management, but if potential CPAs were screened for their ability to handle money, I never would have been accepted as an accounting major. I've been a disaster with money. I never thought about repaying the loans I took out. I never analyzed whether or not I really needed the money. I got as much money as I could and spent it. Now, twelve years later I'm still paying off my debts.

The first lesson I learned *was not to try keeping up with my peers. I had a group of friends who had more money available to them than I did. I thought I had to keep up with them to be accepted. It never occurred to me that we could be friends without me spending money the way they did.*

I joined a sorority—an expense that wasn't in my budget. I made some wonderful friends, but they had a lot more money than I did. We ate out often, which meant I was paying for meals at the sorority house as well as restaurants. We loved movies and often went to clubs, which took another chunk of money I hadn't planned on spending. Then I needed a different wardrobe so I would fit in. It was a huge expense. I learned how to shop for nice things from my sorority sisters and how to live the good life, but I ignored my financial reality.

My solution was to apply for student loans. I also collected as many credit cards as I could—I had eight by the end of my first year. I could have gotten a job during the school year to cover some of these additional expenses, but I was afraid it would cut into my social time. And to be perfectly honest, I thought my friends would look down on me if I worked.

I had not planned to take a trip during my freshman spring break, but all my friends were flying to Mexico, and I desperately wanted to go with them. That's when I discovered university emergency funds. I found out I could borrow up to $1,800 for sixty days and I made a beeline for the office. Mexico was beautiful.

By the end of the school year, I knew I had to make extra money during the summer to pay off some of my debts. I found a second job and thought I would use those earnings to erase my credit card debt. It didn't work out. By fall, I had hardly made a dent in my obligations, so I signed up for more student loans. I didn't give it a single thought. I filled out the paperwork and looked forward to fun times with my sorority sisters.

Later on, I realized I tend to want things now and plan to pay for them sometime in the future, that I will somehow earn or receive money to cover my purchases. It's like knowing you're getting a cash gift for your birthday and spending it over and over again before the money arrives.

Since I was always short of cash, I charged the entire meal when we went out to eat, and my sorority sisters gave me cash for their portion of the bill. I used my credit cards at the ATMs. I didn't realize that a higher interest rate was charged against a cash advance—it was over 22 percent interest. I probably paid more in interest than I originally charged on my credit cards.

I continued to apply for and receive student loans. I never thought ahead about repaying the loans, never considered what that would mean in monthly budgeting or even if I would be able to pay it back. I had this idea that the university was protecting me. I thought they wouldn't give me the loan money if I couldn't repay. I didn't understand my obligation to take responsibility for my debt decisions.

It's hard to believe that I could have been so naïve and simple-minded about these things. But it happened, and twelve years later I'm still living with the consequences.

My out-of-control spending went on for two years until I decided to get married. I had a beautiful wedding with my sorority sisters in attendance. I decided that I would drop out of school and work until Brian finished his degree. It never occurred to me that my student loans would come due six months after I left school. Talk about denial. What an upheaval that caused at home when I started getting the bills.

After some big arguments, Brian and I sat down and listed every debt, the interest rate, and the monthly payment. It was staggering. I had $25,000 of debt in student loans and credit cards. I was earning barely enough to make ends meet and send Brian to school. There simply wasn't enough money to cover the monthly student loan and the credit card payments.

We felt completely stymied—we didn't know what to do. Finally, I talked it over with my parents to see if they could help us.

They were stunned by the amount of debt I had. They had no idea I could get that much money without their knowledge. They told me to go to my financial aid counselor at the university and ask for advice. They also suggested I cut up all my credit cards.

I couldn't cut them up. I needed the financial security the cards gave me. Brian convinced me to get rid of all but one credit card, which he put in a safe place. At least I knew I had it, it just wasn't as accessible. I started using a check card that deducts automatically from the checking account. I still had tremendous urges to spend money, but I noticed that using the equivalent of cash made a difference in how I felt about buying things. I evaluated purchases more carefully, knowing the money would come right out of checking.

Fortunately, my parents kept us afloat for three months until we could figure out what to do. My financial aid counselor warned me that if I ever wanted to get back in school again or transfer, I would have to be careful to make regular payments on my student loans. I didn't realize that if I got behind on my payments the university could deny me admission and withhold my transcript if I tried to transfer to another college.

Brian and I talked about declaring bankruptcy. *I thought it might be the best way to stabilize our situation. The stress on our marriage was incredible. I learned bankruptcy wouldn't erase the student loans and that I would still be responsible for paying them. Brian and I decided we had a moral obligation to repay all our debts.*

I went to the Consumer Credit Counseling office for assistance, and they helped me work out a reasonable repayment schedule on the credit cards and told me how to contact creditors to negotiate monthly payments we could manage. My parents reluctantly agreed to handle the student loan payments until I could pay them. I got a second job and Brian worked as well.

Our financial burdens overwhelmed our marriage. We were only twenty years old and unequipped emotionally to handle it. We sought a counselor at the university for help in our marriage, but when I got pregnant a year later, the relationship became more and more strained. We finally separated when Madison was six months old.

It's been tough, but I'm getting back on my feet financially and emotionally. I managed to get a college degree this year by working and going to school part-time. If I'm careful for the next ten years, I'll be free of debt by the time I'm forty. Now that I have a better-paying job, I pay with cash and I'm careful not to add any more debt. I only borrow money for my car, and one day I hope to buy a house.

I have not had an easy life since I got into debt *and I worry that Madison won't have all the things I would like to give her. She will be going to college around the time I finally get out of debt, and, believe me, I'll be sure she understands how to manage her money before she leaves home.*

A PENCHANT FOR SPENDING

There is a lot to learn from Lesley's story. The first lesson is that a student has to get comfortable with her financial status and grounded in herself as a person. Lesley is not the first person who spent money she did not have in order to impress others. But what a price she paid. She is now thirty and still paying for things she bought as a student. And she doesn't have any prospect of relief for another ten years.

I have seen people fall into this spending mode like they are sliding down a slippery bank into a pond. No matter what they do, they can't seem to climb out of the water. The reason they can't get out is because they can't stop spending. They complain about their lack of discipline, they worry a lot about their debt, they even envision themselves on the street when they are old and unable to work, but they do not stop spending.

If you have this penchant for spending, now—while you are young and relatively debt-free—is the time to conquer this inclination. You will know if you have a problem by the way you spent your money while in high school. If you find that you spent all your money, even though you knew you needed to save for college, that is one sign. If you have a feeling of excitement when you spend, only to be followed by feelings of remorse, that is another indicator. If your friends remark on all the things you have compared to them, maybe you should take a look at your collection of possessions.

CONQUER SPENDING COMPULSIONS

How can you come to grips with your spending compulsions? Study how and when your spending gets out of control. Are there certain conditions that lead to excesses? Perhaps you are bored or worried and shopping relieves that feeling. Instead of buying an item, ask the salesclerk to hold it for twenty-four hours. This will give you time to cool off and reconsider your decision. If you bought the item and now believe it was a mistake, return it to the store.

If you can't control use of your credit cards, cancel them. Use a check or debit card instead of a credit card. Keep the credit limits on your credit cards low until you know you can control your spending. Look for other ways to curb your spending. Ask your parents and friends what they do.

Make an appointment with a counselor at the student health center. Professional counselors can help you explore the reasons for your spending and can assist you in finding ways to change your behavior.

FUTURE MONEY

The second lesson: understand the mind games Lesley played on herself. She always thought she could pay for her purchases in the future by getting another job or using birthday money. She admits she spent future money more than once and her debt kept mounting. This compulsion to spend can be addictive—very difficult to stop or control—and Lesley was hooked. Remember her reluctance to cut up her credit cards. She could not do it. She had to have one card available just in case the urge to spend returned.

It is so easy to talk yourself into spending future money. For example, if you have a tax refund coming for $600, it usually takes about six weeks from the time the tax return is mailed to the Internal Revenue Service until the check arrives in the mail. Six weeks can feel like a lifetime, and it is easy to get excited about a $600 windfall and dream about spending the refund now to bring immediate satisfaction into your life.

You feel entitled to something special, so you buy a new spring wardrobe using a credit card or cash that is needed later in the school year. You know the refund check is coming, and you plan to replace the money at that time. A few weeks later, the check arrives. With the heady prospect of having extra money in hand, you spend the refund a second time.

If you have the inclination to spend future real or imagined funds, acknowledge this tendency and promise you won't spend the money until you have it in hand. Think of this not as denying yourself, but protecting yourself.

It can be difficult to resist spending, but if you can devise a plan to manage your money and follow the strategy for a few months, you will detect a change in your behavior. You will notice a feeling of being in control instead of wildly rushing off to spend anticipated funds. You will lose those feelings of remorse. You will feel grounded around money and steadier in managing your financial life.

KNOW THE RULES

Lesley's third lesson was to monitor her student loans and

understand the rules of repayment. She dropped out of school without thinking that the loans would have to start being repaid if she were not attending classes. She learned that not making the monthly payment could affect her ability to return to school later on. And she discovered there was no escape from the loans—she couldn't declare bankruptcy to get rid of them. Her only option was to negotiate a lower payment that she could meet or go back to school so that the loans would be deferred until she graduated from college and got a better-paying job. That's a lot of pressure for anyone to endure.

Lesley had no idea how much she owed or what her monthly payment would be. I recently talked with a student loan officer who said that students consistently underestimate the total loan money they have borrowed. Even though students may have thousands of dollars of debt in student loans, the number they know, almost to the penny, is how much available credit is on their credit cards. I think the reason for this is that student loans are deferred for payment, but credit cards are in the present; the students receive monthly credit card statements and watch how much credit is still available.

Some universities are encouraging students to make payments on their student loans while they are still in school. This method keeps an awareness of the amount borrowed in the students' minds.

KEEPING TRACK

There are several reasons for keeping track of your student loans. First of all, there is a limit to the total debt you can borrow against governmental sources. I recently heard a story about a fourth-year medical student who had maxed out her loan money by the end of her third year. She had no idea how she was going to finish her program, and she had close to $200,000 in debt to repay. If you keep a running total of your loans, you can be sure not to exceed the limit. Look at the worksheets provided in chapter 6. Ask your financial aid officer what the borrowing limit is for your baccalaureate degree. Write that number in red ink at the top of the Loan Summary worksheet so that you will always be aware of your limit.

Review your loan status before the new academic year starts. Could you manage with less student loan money than the year before? The less you borrow, the less you will have to repay. And if you find at midyear you underestimated your financial need, many loans permit additional funding during the year to make up a shortfall.

It is a good idea to keep the monthly payment you will be required to make on your student loans in your mind as you approach graduation and job hunting. If you use the simple forms provided in this book, you will always know your total debt and the monthly payments. This knowledge will help you decide how much more you are willing to assume in debt each year and how much you can afford. You will be able to compare monthly take-home pay in your chosen profession to the amount of monthly debt repayment you are assuming.

Remember this useful rule of thumb: Your total monthly debt payments, including student loans, car loans, and other personal loans, should never exceed 10 to 15 percent of your take-home pay.

VISUALIZE THE FUTURE

If you can keep your borrowing to a minimum while in college, you will have a lot more money when you reach the work world and want to start buying a home, car, furniture, and a secure future. By limiting your debt, you will have more freedom to pursue your dreams, and you will have options. You won't be stuck in a job you discover you do not like but cannot leave because you have too many financial restrictions. That is what debt is—a restriction on your life.

Getting a college education is a good investment, even if you have to borrow money to achieve it. But be careful not to take on frivolous debt. Do not fund a new wardrobe with student loan money. You will be paying for it years after you get your college degree.

FINANCIAL BASICS

- Teach yourself how to spend money on important things for yourself, not to spend money to impress others or to make friends.
- Have the courage to say "I can't afford this."
- Be aware of your overall student loan amount even if you are not making monthly payments.
- Find out immediately the terms for repaying all student loans—when repayment must begin.
- If you are having trouble with spending, seek out a counselor
- When you manage your spending, you are not denying yourself. You are protecting yourself.

6

How Much Did You Say I Owed?

YOU WILL GET a lot of information from the student financial aid office at your chosen college or university. There will be helpful counselors to guide you through the work of applying for student aid and loans. There is another important office on campus that you will not have contact with until you leave school: the collections office, which is responsible for collecting most student loans when they come due.

Debbie worked in her university's collections office during her college years. She likes to joke that she got a Ph.D. in personal finance working in this office and hearing stories about the financial problems former students were having with their loans.

DEBBIE'S STORY

I got a wake-up call when I started working in the collections office my freshman year. The collections office mails notices to students, receives payments, follows up on delinquent loans, talks with and counsels student debtors, and turns over uncollectible loans to debt-collection agencies.

As I heard stories of students when they came to the office to complain or ask for help, I realized that I better be more careful about my own student loan situation. This work experience forced me to think about how much debt I was taking on and how I was going to repay it.

I can't tell you how many people *came into the office insisting they did not have to repay their loans because they didn't get a job in their field. They were angry and upset. These people felt they should have been warned. They wondered why in the world they were ever approved for such high loan amounts when the job market was limited in their field.*

Some graduates were distraught because their monthly loan repayment swallowed such a big portion of their budget. They were unable to qualify for a mortgage because of their high monthly debt payments. They questioned why they were allowed to take on so much debt.

That's when I began to comprehend that students get loans based on their financial need while in school, not on their ability to repay after they leave school. No other type of loan is made in this way. An installment loan or a home mortgage is always based on the earning power of the borrower. I think that's why it's confusing to some students and sometimes their parents.

It was disturbing to observe the number of students who didn't comprehend what they had taken on when they got loans. Some didn't understand that interest would be added to their loans. Some students didn't realize they were receiving money that had to be repaid. Then we encountered the occasional student who had trouble finishing the last few terms because she had borrowed the maximum allowable and didn't have enough money to complete her degree program. When I met her, I started keeping careful track of all my loans. I didn't want to get caught in a situation where I wouldn't have enough money to finish school.

The biggest, lasting impression *for me was what a burden loan payments imposed on many of the people who came to our office. I realized that I had better look ahead. I needed to figure my earnings potential when I got my degree. My major was social work. I understood that social workers didn't make big salaries, but I didn't know exact salaries. I went online to find starting compensation levels, estimated my take-home pay, and kept a running total on what my required monthly loan payment would be after I left school. I wanted to be sure that my total monthly payment did not exceed 10 percent of my take-home pay. I wasn't comfortable with anything higher.*

By keeping track and monitoring my debt level, I borrowed less money than I ordinarily would have, and five years after getting my degree I'm very thankful that I limited myself. It means that I can take vacations, save for a house, and contribute fully to my retirement plan. Being knowledgeable also made me more confident in my financial-handling practices. I didn't worry about money as long as I stayed within the parameters I set up for myself.

When the collections office failed to collect *loans, the accounts were turned over to debt-collection agencies. These agencies work aggressively to collect monies owed to the university and government, and they usually get paid one-third of everything they bring in. Professional debt collectors are tough; I wouldn't want to be on the other end of a phone call from one of them. The person who ran our department fiercely pursued collections, but she had a heart, too. She trained our staff to listen to the debtors—really listen—and try to help students, but the bottom line was to do our best to collect the debt.*

Observing the collection process, I learned that if a person runs into trouble repaying loans, it is in his best interest to immediately contact the lender and discuss the problem. Most lenders seem willing to work with genuine problems. It saves them money they would have spent finding the debtor, and it saves the debtor a lot of nasty mail and phone calls—not to mention the stress of worrying about the situation.

I was surprised at the consequences *of students not repaying debt after they leave school. If a student drops out for six or nine months, most loans will no longer be deferred and the borrower will have to start repaying the debt. Sometimes a former student can't make the monthly payments. If he or she quits making monthly payments, the loan will be considered in default and the borrower will not be able to get a transcript from the school and will not be able to reenter or transfer to another school until he or she clears the previous loans. Federal income tax refunds may be confiscated to pay down the debt and employers may be required to send a portion of the person's wages to the loan agency (it's called garnishing wages). Even if the former student declares bankruptcy, his or her student loan will remain on file and it still will have to be repaid.*

Sometimes student borrowers would move to a new place or a new town and neglect to notify all their creditors. I can't tell you the number of times students thought if they told one university office of their new address, everyone would have access to the change. Information is not shared. Students must send address changes to all creditors. Even if a borrower doesn't receive her mail (perhaps it was lost or stolen), she risks being in default on a loan. I also learned that students don't always open their mail! This is a big mistake. Even if you don't deal with your mail you are still responsible for your loan—it doesn't disappear.

My advice to prospective student borrowers? *Make sure you understand the loan provisions, keep a running total of how much you have borrowed, and what your monthly repayment amount will be. And don't take on any more debt than you have to borrow to get through school.*

KEEPING TRACK

Debbie makes a convincing case for being aware of what you are getting into when you start taking out student loans. This does not mean you should not borrow to get an education. It is a good investment, and you should be able to recover your investment by earning a higher salary than if you did not earn a college degree. But there are some cautionary lessons in Debbie's story.

Make a commitment to keep an inventory of all your loans. Here is a form that I suggest you use. Create a file or a notebook to store all your loan information. Put the Student Loan Inventory Master List in the front of the file and update it every term.

Completing the Student Loan Inventory Master List will provide the pertinent information of every loan in one convenient place. If you need to contact your lenders for any reason, you will have easy access to your information. Notice that the fourth line concerns interest. Most federally backed student loans do not start adding interest costs to the loan until the student leaves school and the loan repayment is activated. Alternative student loans start adding interest to the loan amount as soon as the account is established, and the interest rate is usually higher than the federally backed loans. This increases the debt more quickly than interest-deferred loans. Try not to take out these early interest-accruing loans until absolutely necessary. For example, if you can delay

Student Loan Inventory Master List

Loan #1

Loan Type _____   Account Number _____

Loan Amount $ _____   Interest Rate _____%

Repayment begins _____   Monthly Payments $ _____

Interest starts accruing: ○ Immediately   ○ At repayment

Loan Holder / Servicer _____

Phone Number _____

- -

Loan #2

Loan Type _____   Account Number _____

Loan Amount $ _____   Interest Rate _____%

Repayment begins _____   Monthly Payments $ _____

Interest starts accruing: ○ Immediately   ○ At repayment

Loan Holder / Servicer _____

Phone Number _____

- -

Loan #3

Loan Type _____   Account Number _____

Loan Amount $ _____   Interest Rate _____%

Repayment begins _____   Monthly Payments $ _____

Interest starts accruing: ○ Immediately   ○ At repayment

Loan Holder / Servicer _____

Phone Number _____

- -

Loan #4

Loan Type _____   Account Number _____

Loan Amount $ _____   Interest Rate _____%

Repayment begins _____   Monthly Payments $ _____

Interest starts accruing: ○ Immediately   ○ At repayment

Loan Holder / Servicer _____

Phone Number _____

borrowing these types of loans until your senior year, the loan will accumulate less interest before you graduate and start repaying the debt.

Loan Summary

Loan #	Repay Starts	Amount Borrowed	Total Amount Borrowed	Monthly Payment	Total Monthly Payment
1					
2					
3					
4					
5					
6					
7					
8					
9					
10					
11					

Behind the Student Loan Inventory Master List in your notebook, keep a running total of the amount of money you have borrowed and the monthly repayment amount. This one-page Loan Summary includes columns for keeping the balances of the total amount borrowed and the monthly payments when the loan is activated for repayment.

By using the Loan Summary you will always know your monthly debt obligation after you leave college. If you set a target amount for monthly payments like Debbie did, you will easily know when you are getting close to your limit. That knowledge will keep you on top of your financial situation, and you will feel in charge. For some people, a lack of knowledge creates a nagging worry that saps energy. With the Loan Summary you won't have that problem.

Debbie was concerned about repaying her student loans on a social worker's salary. She did a smart thing by acquiring starting salary information for her profession in the towns she was interested in living. This information is available in the library or on the Internet from the Bureau of Labor Statistics (http://www.bls.gov). Look in the *Occupational Handbook* or the *Occupational Employment Statistics.* Consult a counselor in your college for additional help to develop this salary number.

Debbie took her calculations a step further. She figured out her take-home pay and tried to estimate her costs of living. It is so easy

Monthly Take-Home Pay			
	Career/City	Career/City	Career/City
Monthly Salary			
Less Payroll Deductions			
Federal Tax (15%)			
FICA (7.6%)			
State Tax*			
City Tax*			
Medical Insurance			
Retirement Contribution			
Disability			
Other			
Take-Home Pay			

* These vary depending on where you live. Find out the exact amounts, or, if you aren't sure where you'll be living, use estimates of 4% and 1% respectively to estimate state and city taxes.

to think of an annual salary and forget to deduct income taxes and other expenses withheld from the paycheck. You can expect at least a 25 to 30 percent reduction in your pay because of various withholdings. There is federal income tax, usually state income tax, often city tax, FICA (Social Security), and Medicare. You may have health insurance, short- or long-term disability insurance, life insurance, and retirement programs deducted from your paycheck.

To project your take-home pay, use the Monthly Take-Home Pay worksheet. Notice that there are three columns. You may be considering more than one profession or contemplating different places to live. Use the columns to look at your options.

PLANNING AHEAD

Debbie had a goal of not exceeding 10 percent of her take-home pay in student loan payments. By getting an estimate of her salary expectations and payroll deductions, she took the first step to assure herself that she could meet this financial requirement. Some financial advisors suggest that total monthly debt repayment,

Monthly Living Expenses

	Career/City	Career/City	Career/City
Rent			
Utilities			
Food			
Transportation			
Student Loan			
Other Loans			
Clothing/Personal Care			
Recreation, Entertainment, Gifts			
Charitable			
Savings			
Total Expenses			
Take-Home Pay			
Take-Home Pay Less Expenses			

including student loans, credit cards, car loans, but not rent or mortgage payments, should not exceed 15 percent of take-home pay and, if you find yourself approaching 20 percent, start working to get some loans paid more quickly. In the final analysis, it is up to you to decide how much debt you want to assume.

Another way to assess your appropriate debt level is to estimate your monthly expenses after you leave school. Use the Monthly Living Expenses worksheet I have provided for you. Start by using your current expenses and adjust the costs according to your best information. For example, you know what your student loan payments will be by using the Loan Summary. Check the classifieds in the newspaper where you plan to live to get an idea of living costs. If you plan to buy a car, estimate the monthly payment plus operating expenses. Plug in 10 percent of your take-home pay in the savings column. When you are finished, add all the expenses, deduct them from your take-home pay, and see if you have any money left.

If you find that your take-home pay will not cover your living expenses, you need to rethink your decisions. There are two basic areas to consider: you either have to make more money or reduce expenses. Could you make more money and be satisfied with your work if you chose another career? If the answer is no, then can you reduce your student loans to a level that allows you to follow your career decision? This might mean living a more moderate life while you are in school or transferring to a less expensive college.

Sit down with a counselor, a wise friend, or a parent to review your thinking. Sometimes another person can come up with ideas that you have not considered. Or, you and your friends could brainstorm possible options; for example, bus transportation might alleviate the pressures of owning and maintaining a car.

Having this information will allow you to make better decisions as you go through college. You will not wake up in the middle of the night wondering if you will have financial problems when you start working. You will not suddenly find yourself in the workforce with burdensome unanticipated debt that restricts your ability to enjoy life.

FINANCIAL BASICS

- Find out when the first repayment of your student loan is due and when interest begins to accrue.
- Keep an ongoing Student Loan Inventory Master List and Loan Summary worksheets to keep track of all student loans.
- If you move to a new town or change your address, notify all lenders.
- Use the Monthly Take-Home Pay and Monthly Living Expenses worksheets.
- Research your future career, find out the potential salary, estimate living expenses and loan payments and subtract these from your take-home pay to see if you are overextending your debt.

7

But Don't I Need to Build a Credit History?

A LITTLE KNOWLEDGE is a dangerous thing. Many students do not realize they are creating a credit history while they are in school. Beth thought she would not have a credit history until she took out a bank loan. She was in for a big surprise when she tried to rent an apartment after graduation.

BETH'S STORY

I'll be honest. I didn't always pay my bills on time when I was in college. I don't know why. I had the money, but I hated writing checks. I told myself I was busy with school—I'd get to it later. So I let my payments slide for a month or so. I received late notices, but the companies didn't seem too upset. I figured it was no big deal. I was actually saving time by only paying my bills every other month. It turned out to be a big deal, but I didn't discover that until I graduated from college.

***I moved to Minneapolis** from Cleveland to start a new job as a business manager with a small college. I hoped to live near the campus and was excited about getting my own apartment.*

I located the perfect place about two miles from the campus and arranged to rent the apartment. I didn't realize that the manager would run a credit check. Two days later, Nancy called. She said I had a history of late payments on some of my bills while I was in college, and she needed a larger deposit than she originally stated. Instead of the first and last months' rent, she required a six-month deposit on my place. If I paid my rent on time for one year, she would return the extra four months' deposit at the end of the year.

I was in shock. Thanks to a generous graduation present from my godmother, I had a start-up fund to get established in Minneapolis. My godmother pointed out that I would have a lot of one-time expenses getting my new life in order like buying a work wardrobe, renting an apartment, making deposits on utilities, and furnishing my new place. A six-month rental deposit would cut my little start-up fund to the bone. I wouldn't be able to furnish my place as I imagined, and I had to scale back my plans for a car and new clothes.

I hated being blindsided *like that, and I made up my mind to find out what I could about my financial records and determine if I could get my record changed. When I opened my new bank account in Minneapolis, I asked the banker how I could get more information. Hazel explained there are three organizations that collect financial data, and I could request a copy of my credit report from these firms:*

1. Experian: (888) 397–3742; www.experian.com
2. Equifax: (800) 685–1111; www.equifax.com
3. TransUnion: (800) 888–4313; www.tuc.com

I was amazed at the amount of information that was already collected on me. Nancy was right. I had been late with my credit card payments and telephone bills. All of my late-payment history appeared in the report. In addition, I had written a bad check once (after that I got overdraft protection for my checking account) and the retailer had reported the bounced check to the credit agency. Plus, all my credit cards were listed. One was an account that I had taken out at a department store during a special promotion and I never used that card again. I even forgot I had that card.

I went back to my helpful banker with the credit report *and asked what I could do to get rid of the negative information. I learned that it could* take up to seven years to clear my credit report. In the meantime, I would be paying higher interest rates for loans because a bank or another creditor reviewing my report would feel I was less likely to repay a loan and that represented more risk to the lender. Hazel was not surprised that my rental deposit had been increased. She said every day a tenant doesn't pay rent costs the landlord money in lost revenue. I was upset, but I pulled myself together and asked Hazel what I should do.

Hazel told me to cancel the credit cards I wasn't using and didn't want. When I asked her why, she replied that even though I might not have any charges on these cards, the fact that credit was available would count against me when I tried to get a loan. Available credit is the same as having debt as far as a lender is concerned.

She suggested sending a letter by certified mail to the credit card company requesting that they cancel my account and to be sure they noted that it was canceled at my request. This would eliminate a canceled credit card showing up in my credit report as though the company had canceled me. A copy of my letter along with the mailing receipt should be placed in my permanent files.

The tough part was clearing my credit report. Hazel explained that even though I would be able to get a loan for the used car I had found, I would end up paying a higher rate of interest because of my poor credit history. She reminded me it could take up to seven years to improve my credit rating and advised me to be patient, to pay my bills on time, and always pay at least the minimum amount required. I was somewhat relieved when she said that some financial institutions looked more carefully at the latest two years of activity rather than the whole history. That made me even more determined to follow Hazel's advice.

It has been four years since I graduated from college, and my apartment is furnished the way I hoped it would be and my car loan is paid. I followed Hazel's advice and made sure to pay my bills on time. I am getting married in a few months, and we plan to buy a house. I hope my credit report will pass a mortgage company's scrutiny.

I wish I had known how much information was being collected on my financial life while I was still in college. I did not realize that I was building a credit history. I would have been a lot more careful if I had known.

CREDIT REPORTS COUNT

While interviewing a group of students who were willing to talk about their financial practices, I met a student who seemed intent on trying all kinds of ways to manage his money. His latest approach was to pay his bills every three months. He said he was too busy to do it more often. He had no idea his behavior was being recorded and might make life more expensive and difficult later on.

Most students though, wonder how and when they should begin to build a credit history. They are aware that a good credit history will be important as they begin to look for jobs, buy cars, and apply for mortgages, and that employers are increasingly accessing credit reports on potential employees as another way of assessing the person's background.

While college students have an awareness of the importance of one's credit rating, the knowledge about the process seems to be lacking. One of the comments I hear frequently from bankers and other financial professionals is that college students are ruining their credit ratings by not paying their bills on time.

In this high-tech age of constant information transfer, much of our financial activity is being recorded in a central data bank. Writing a bad check or skipping a monthly payment is very likely to appear in a financial record. Even inadvertently closing a bank account without sufficient funds to cover outstanding checks will probably show up in your records. This kind of negative information might lead a bank to refuse giving you a new account. Imagine not being able to open a checking account.

THE BEST WAY

The basic lesson from Beth's story is pay your bills on time and be cautious about getting credit cards. It is a good idea to get a copy of your credit report annually to be sure it is correct and to know what information is in it. If you are ever refused credit because of one of these agencies' reports, you can request a free copy of your report from them. If they have an error in your file, you can get it corrected.

Having a credit card and paying it off every month will help establish your good credit. And having good credit will enable you to get lower interest rates on loans such as automobile loans when you graduate from college. The tricky part about credit cards is being able to control them—not let them take over your desire for consumption.

If you have any doubts about your ability to control your credit card spending, do not get one. Wait a year or so until you have the self-control to manage a credit card. Another alternative is to get a card with a low credit limit. This will prevent you from accumulating thousands of dollars of debt like so many other students have done. With a low credit limit, you can practice using your credit card, pay attention to the way you use the card and begin to understand your financial nature. You may have certain triggers that cause you to spend money without thinking, or you may delay paying your bills for some reason. This is the time to think about why you do this and look for solutions to manage your inclinations. Don't berate yourself for your particular way of handling money. Learn and grow from your experiences.

Do not accept offers to raise your credit limit unless you have a good reason for wanting the higher limit. When offered the increased line of credit, write the company asking that the limit you set be maintained. Keep a copy of that letter in your permanent files in case you need to prove later that it was your decision, not the credit card company's.

SMART BORROWING

Once you are working full-time you will have more leverage for getting better interest rates. For example, if you do have balances on your credit cards that you are slowly paying off, try to get one of the credit card companies to give you a lower interest rate and consolidate all your debt on that card. You may be able to negotiate better terms if you do all your business and have a history with one financial institution. Always ask if the lender can give you a more favorable interest rate when you are negotiating a loan.

Pay attention to general interest rates such as the prime rate. If the prime starts going down, you may be able to renegotiate your rate on your credit cards (if you are carrying balances). Always remember, though, credit cards are generally the most expensive debt there is.

I recently interviewed two young bank managers—recent college graduates—who work in offices near a university campus. I asked them what they thought were the most prevalent financial issues facing university students. They both told me three things that college students needed to be aware of:

1. Calling the bank for the checking account balance does not mean the student can write checks for that amount. The student needs to understand that checks usually don't clear the bank for two or three days.
2. College students are ruining their credit by not paying their bills on time.
3. Credit cards are dangerous.

Remember to balance your checkbook every month so that you know how much money you have. See chapter 4 to refresh your memory about checkbook reconciliation. If you are concerned about your balance, access your account online, and quickly balance your checkbook to the current date. Don't rely on the bank to provide an answer to your cash balance. Checks and debit card charges usually take two or three days after the transaction to show up in your account. Deposits, unless they are cash, also take several days to clear, so be sure to wait to write checks on that deposit.

Always pay your bills on time. If you have a problem, write to the payee explaining your problem and what you plan to do in order to pay your bill.

Pay your credit card bill in full every month. You do not have to maintain debt on your credit card to build a credit history.

BANKERS' PERSONAL STORIES

I didn't ask how these two young bank managers had handled their own money during their college years, but much to my surprise, the conversation quickly turned personal in both interviews. Both of these men told me they did not carry a credit card anymore.

They had credit cards while in school, but their spending got out of hand. Now that they were out of school with full-time jobs, they were trying to get out of debt. Both of them had cut up their cards until they could pay them off and gain confidence about managing a credit card.

Bruce started out with a credit card from his parents' credit union. The card was in his and his parents' names with a generous credit line based on his parents' history. After a few years, he received his own card, but the credit line remained high—$12,000. Bruce, a musician, did not get his degree in four years. He was twenty-six when he graduated from college, and he had used the credit card to fund his expenses while he alternately pursued a music career and an education. After graduating, he hoped to find a job as a music teacher in the public school system, but teaching jobs were not available, so he began working for a bank. Since he was working for a financial institution, he made a point of learning about sound fiscal management. He cut up his card and concentrated on paying off the debt.

Jim said that he didn't know he had a problem with debt until one day Don, the older brother of his best friend, talked about how to handle money. Don showed Jim how much interest he was paying on his credit cards and helped Jim develop a plan to pay them off. Jim felt he had been illiterate about debt and immediately started to pay off the card with the highest interest rate. He explained that it didn't make sense to increase the monthly payment on each of his cards (he had five credit cards with balances), but to choose the most expensive one and pay it off first while paying the minimum on the other cards.

After Jim cut up his credit cards, he used a check card instead. He logged on to his bank account every morning to double-check the entries in his checkbook and balance his account. This strategy eliminated the "big" job of balancing his checkbook once a month, which he said he avoided because it overwhelmed him. By checking the entries every morning, he never missed any of his check card charges, as he had in the past.

Both Bruce and Jim feel so strongly about informing students about the dangers of credit cards that they personally counsel students who are building up debt by sharing their mistakes. They believe they now help other students understand the issues around credit cards, how to get out of debt, and how to stay out of debt.

I was surprised by these two men's disclosures—not that they had incurred credit card debt while in college, but their strong desire to pass on their personal experiences to other students so that current students wouldn't make the same mistakes. It was as if they were on a mission.

LOOK FOR OPTIONS

If you have difficulty paying your bills on time, look for solutions to enable you to keep your credit rating strong. Many organizations will automatically deduct a payment from your checking account each month. This will ensure that your payment is always on time.

There are several ways to pay bills online. Some banks offer this service and some companies will allow you to set up a mechanism for paying their bill online. Querying your balance online is particularly useful with credit cards. You will learn how much you have charged and if you are nearing your ability to pay off the balance, you can back off using the card.

Try paying your bills as soon as you receive your statement. It will seem easier to get the bills paid if you divide the work into smaller segments. Paying your bills as soon as you receive them will make you feel more powerful about your money.

Personal accounting software packages, such as Microsoft Money or Quicken, are available to track financial data, print checks, and import bank data to balance your checking account. They provide reminders for routine payments such as rent or telephone bills.

DISCLOSURE

Beth is getting married in a few months. Should she tell her fiancé about her financial history? Absolutely. This is not something a partner wants revealed after a few months of marriage and it *will* be exposed when they apply for a mortgage. Undisclosed or unresolved money issues can be devastating to a marriage. Both partners need to share their current and past financial data. This is a good starting point to establish how to handle money as a couple. If there are disagreements about personal finances, it is wise to consult a counselor or financial professional about money-handling options and come to agreement on how to set up the financial arrangements that are fair to both people.

FINANCIAL BASICS

- Pay your bills on time and if you need to make other arrangements, contact your creditors.
- As an adult, be conscious of the fact that you are building a credit history. Companies are charting your paying patterns, debt, and credit limits.
- Request a copy of your credit history before you graduate from college to ensure there are no erroneous entries.
- If you move, be sure you submit your address change to all lenders and your bank.

8

Car Crazy

HAVING A CAR on campus—it sounds ideal. Think of the freedom. Jump in the car anytime you want to go somewhere or take your friends out on the weekends to a restaurant or new club. When you start to dream about having a car on campus, it is hard to imagine how you would get along without it. But, of course, like everything in life, there is another side to consider before heading to the car dealer. There are the financial aspects of owning a car.

RON'S STORY

I loved my car. I took good care of my car, changed the oil regularly, made sure it was clean and polished. It was a shiny black used Rover with dark-gray leather interior, and I loved cruising around campus. I thought I could afford the Rover, but I badly miscalculated.

My mom tried to talk me out of getting a car *before I went to college, but I'd had this dream since I was little, and I wasn't going to let it go. Mom worried a car would cost too much money while I was in college. But once I owned the car I figured out a budget for college including the car expenses. It was tight, but I knew all the costs: gas, insurance, and maintenance. My dad said the car was in good shape, so I was certain* there wouldn't be too much expense beyond normal maintenance, most of which I planned to do myself. I was convinced I could manage all right.

I was right. It was great having a car. I made a lot of good friends, and I always drove when we went out. Sometimes they would ask me to take them places to run errands or take them home for the weekend, and I was happy to help out. It was cool to have so many friends during my freshman year.

The problem was I was beginning to run short on money. I thought I had everything figured out, but by the end of the first term, I knew I had messed up my calculations. There were costs I had not even thought about when I set up my budget. First of all, I had to pay to park my car on campus, a quarterly fee of $75. Not a lot of money, but I hadn't put it in my already tight budget. Sometimes when I was running behind schedule and didn't want to be late for class, I'd park at a meter or in a closer parking lot. I got a lot of tickets. I couldn't believe it. A ticket at an expired meter cost $10, and if I parked in the wrong lot I found a $25 ticket on my windshield. I tried to pay them, but sometimes I didn't have the money so I tossed the ticket in a drawer, thinking I would pay it later.

I'll never forget walking down to the parking lot one Saturday night with my friends. We had planned a big night. When we got to the lot I couldn't locate my car. I thought it was stolen, and when I called the campus police they informed me the car had been impounded because of all my parking tickets. I had to get a ride to the impound lot and pay all the tickets, plus towing costs and the impound fee. It came to $350. I had the money, but it wiped me out for the rest of the quarter. When I called home for more money, Mom told me they couldn't spare it and I'd have to figure out something else. At least she didn't say, "I told you so."

A friend told me about the university emergency loan fund and I borrowed $350, but I had to pay it back by the beginning of the next quarter. I asked for more hours at the bookstore where I worked part-time. Working extra hours took time away from my studies, and my grades slipped. My scholarship contract said I had to maintain a certain grade average to continue to receive money.

I started to get a little nervous about all these problems when I got a letter from a credit card company saying I was approved for a $500 line *of credit. I felt good—like some bank thought I was trustworthy. This might be the answer. I signed up right away and started using the card. I cut back my work hours. I had things under control again.*

When the beginning of the next quarter rolled around, it was time to pay off the emergency loan. I had planned to use a cash advance from the credit card to pay the loan, but I didn't have enough availability in my credit line. In fact, I had charged over $400 on the card, a little more than the cost of getting my car out of hock. I'm not sure where that money went.

I walked by a table in the student union where a bank was offering a free T-shirt along with a credit card, and I signed up. It was so easy. They told me they would send me blank checks I could use as if it were my checking account. The only difference was the money would be charged on my credit card as a cash advance. I used this check to pay off the university loan. I was a little uneasy about taking on another credit card, but hey, I didn't see what else I could do. My car expenses were a lot higher than I'd planned. I didn't realize how many miles I'd be putting on the car. I spent a lot on gas, changed the oil more often, and when I hit a big pothole, I had to replace one of the tires.

I went home for the summer and landed a job with a manufacturing company in town. It was hot, heavy work, but it paid better than anything else I could find, and I hoped to get some overtime work. I had to make as much money as I could during the summer break.

My mom noticed that I was getting bills *from credit card companies and asked me what was going on. I explained that I had figured out how to get the extra money to cover my car problems by using the credit cards. She was surprised and upset. My parents don't have a lot of money, and it worried her that I was getting into debt even before I began a full-time job.*

That night my parents and I discussed my debt. I had $1,000 in charges on my credit cards. As my mom pointed out, I had spent $1,000 more than I planned for my first year in college. I realized that if I kept going at this rate, I would have $4,000 in debt when I graduated from college. My mom corrected my calculations.

"Look Ron, when you graduate you will have $4,000 in debt, plus the interest you are being charged on your balances. Making the minimum monthly payment will hardly put a dent in the debt. And when you took a cash advance they charged you an even higher rate of interest. You are

paying 15 percent interest on your purchases and 22 percent on that cash advance you took to pay off the university emergency loan. It's like a runaway train of additional costs."

She pointed out that the minimum monthly payment is based on a ten-year repayment schedule, and I would probably pay at least that much more in interest. To be honest, I hadn't even thought about the cost of borrowing money, and this was one fast, painful lesson on the power of compound interest.

My mom addressed another problem. I needed to look at how much money I would need to live on campus next year and how I would pay for it. I earn $4,000 from my summer job and part-time work, my parents chip in another $5,000, and my scholarship is $1,000. So that's $10,000, but it looked like I needed $11,000 a year to cover all my expenses. With a sinking feeling, I knew the answer to my budget problem. I would have to give up my car.

Then I had an inspiration. My parents and I had tried to make my undergraduate educational funding work without borrowing student loan money, but now it made more sense to borrow money that I wouldn't have to pay back until I graduated from college. The interest rate would be a lot lower than the credit card rates, too.

Dad reminded me that I had planned a strategy for paying for my undergraduate degree so I could continue on to professional school. My original game plan was that I would not borrow any money, other than the car loan, until I went into dentistry. I knew dentistry would cost a bundle—probably around $30,000 a year—and I would have to borrow at least $20,000 a year. It seemed smart to keep my costs as low as possible while I was an undergraduate, because I knew later I was going to take on big debt.

Then my dad really blew me away. He said, "As I see it, the problem is that you want to finance your car twice."

He went on to say that if I borrowed student loan money, I'll have a $4,000 debt just for operating the car. I won't be debt-free when I graduate from college. In fact, I won't finish paying for the Rover until after I start working as a dentist because the repayment schedule will be deferred until I finish dental school.

Why would I want to borrow money to drive a car I couldn't afford and start paying off that loan in six years when I might not even have the *original car? I realized that it was better to give up my car now and wait until I had extra income.*

I sold the car at a $2,500 loss, but with no car payments and other related expenses I was able to cover the loss and pay off the credit card balance in less than a year.

I missed my Rover. But I kept telling myself someday I would have an even finer car. And it was a relief not to be so worried about stretching my money to cover all my expenses.

Now I am in my last year of dental school, and I'm glad I didn't waste student loan funds on a car. I borrowed a lot of money to go to dental school, but that's an investment in the work I want to do. An investment that I will recoup by earning a good living and doing work that I enjoy.

Like I said, one day I'll get the car of my dreams. In the meantime, I still have a credit card because it is convenient, but I always pay the full balance every month. Actually, it feels good to write a check for the balance due. I'm in charge—not my credit cards or my car.

EMOTION VERSUS FACT

Emotions play a big role in the way we handle money. Sometimes we want something so much that we subconsciously skew our information gathering so that we can have what we want immediately. Ron's love of cars and his strong desire to have a certain image overtook his innate common sense.

You will notice that Ron did not figure out his spending plan until after he bought the car. He believed that somehow he would make his money cover the extra costs of owning a car. When he drew up a spending plan, he realized that money would be tight— but he left no room for error in his plan.

Ron had another problem: he did not know the full costs of owning a car. As he developed estimates of the costs of getting a higher education, he needed to go to multiple sources for complete information. The costs for parking a car on campus are in a list of fees that the university provides. Reading that list carefully for any fees he might incur and talking with other experienced people about the costs of owning a car at college would have informed him of expenses he had not considered.

EMERGENCY FUND

Ron did not take into account emergencies and unforeseen events. There are two things he could have done to protect himself. First, he needed to add an amount to his spending plan for flexibility. It is very difficult to construct a precise spending plan. You always need to build in a little extra money to cover the unknown. By doing this, you will make a better-informed decision on whether your desired purchase is really possible within your income.

Ron also needed an emergency fund—some money put aside in a savings account that he touched only in an emergency. The blown-out tire qualifies as an emergency. The ongoing parking tickets and subsequent impounded-car costs qualify as emergencies too, but he could have avoided the onslaught of tickets after receiving the first one.

It is hard to have an emergency fund when money is tight, but if at all possible try to set aside $250 to $500 for this purpose, even if you don't have a car. One source of emergency funds might be an income tax refund. Commit to putting your tax refund check aside for emergencies. It will give you a feeling of security and prevent you from using costly cash advances from your credit card or borrowing from other sources.

If you are afraid you will be tempted to spend the extra money in your emergency fund, put the money in a separate account or in another bank that is not quite as accessible. Alternatively, open another account at your bank that requires two signatures for withdrawals—you and another trustworthy person who will help you decide if your withdrawal truly qualifies as an emergency.

LOOK AT THE OPTIONS

Ron could have asked himself the question, "What will happen if I don't have a car on campus?" This was a tough question for Ron to entertain. He really wanted that car. But it is a good question to ask yourself whenever you are considering any purchase that is nonessential and may put stress on your finances.

Ron could have decided to wait a year before he bought a car. Living on a residential campus usually reduces the need for personal transportation. Other modes of transportation, such as public transportation or a bicycle might have been adequate. As far as trips home, the cost of a bus, train, or plane tickets might have been a lot less than the cost of a car over nine months of school.

These options for transportation are not always apparent until one is living in the actual situation. If Ron had waited until the end of his first year, he would have a lot more knowledge to make a decision.

EVALUATING LOANS

Some students believe that it is okay to take on debt for extras while in college because they will be earning good money when they graduate. If you get into this habit, I can guarantee you that you will always have debt. There will always be some source of future funds to anticipate: a raise, a birthday check, an income tax refund, an inheritance.

Money borrowed to invest in your education makes sense. You are investing in yourself, and the average college graduate earns about 50 percent more over a lifetime than a high school graduate. If you need to borrow money to pay tuition and basic living costs while in college, that is a reasonable investment. Student loans are usually at lower interest rates and often do not start accruing interest until after you graduate.

It is wise to consider the long-term effects regarding your financial decisions. Ask yourself if you want to be paying for your college car years after you have bought a new car (and taken out a loan for the new car). And, if you do, ask yourself if you really want to use student loans or expensive credit cards to fund the car expenses. In many cases, a car purchase is not an allowable use of student loan funds.

CAN'T AFFORD TO SELL THE CAR

Some students caught in a financial bind say they can't afford to sell their car because they will take a loss. That is not really true. If the student considered the savings generated by eliminating the car payment, insurance, gas, and maintenance, the loss would be recouped over time. If you are struggling to make ends meet, gather the facts and examine the possibilities.

Add up all the money you spend each month on the car. Don't forget to include the monthly cost of insurance and any other additional costs that are paid less frequently like the license.

Find out how much it would cost to pay off the car loan and the current market value of your car. Subtract the car loan from the market value. If you have a gain or break even, selling the car will relieve your finances immediately.

If you have a loss, divide the loss by the monthly costs. The result is the number of months it will take to break even. In Ron's case he had to cover a $2,500 loss on the sale of the car, but he saved $400 a month in car payments and operating expenses. It took a little over six months ($2,500 divided by $400) for him to break even. Ron borrowed $2,500 from his bank. His father co-signed the loan. After he repaid the loan, Ron had $400 extra a month, which he saved for dental school.

LEASING

Leasing is attractive when on a limited budget because the monthly payments are less. But before you sign a lease, educate yourself on the particulars. The reason lease payments are generally lower than car loan payments is because you are paying for the use of a car over a certain time frame. The leasing company owns the car and estimates the value at the end of the lease period (usually four years). The lease cost (what you pay) covers the difference between the full price of the car and the residual value of the car at the end of the lease, plus interest.

Before you sign a lease contract, remember that you are committed to making those payments for the entire time period. If you decide you can't afford the car midway into the lease, you will have to arrange with the leasing company to sell the car. You will probably pay a stiff penalty for breaking the lease, and you will have to cover any loss associated with the sale. And this assumes that the car can be sold. When the economy slowed down in the high-tech sector, car lots were full of leased cars waiting to be sold because the lessee had lost his or her job and couldn't afford the car. The lessee had to continue the monthly payments until the car was sold.

Take into account the restriction on the number of miles you can put on the car during the lease period. It's usually ten to fifteen thousand miles a year, and if you exceed that restriction there will be additional costs to pay when you return the car at the end of the lease.

If you decide to lease, ask what interest rate is used to compute the lease payment. Compare that number to car loan interest. If the lease interest is higher, try to negotiate a lower rate. It doesn't hurt to ask.

EVALUATE PURCHASES

Train yourself to step back and think about the purchases you are making that are not critical to your pursuit of a degree. If you are borrowing money for a purchase, especially student loan money, ask yourself if you want to be paying for this item long after you graduate from college. If you learn to manage your purchases, you can stem a flow of debt that may creep into your way of life forever.

FINANCIAL BASICS

- Before making a big purchase of a car for college, analyze costs for gas, licensing, insurance, maintenance, parking, and emergency situations such as parking tickets or new tires.
- Explore other transportation options at your school.
- Don't finance short-term, nonessential purchases with student loan money.
- If you have made a mistake in buying a nonessential item, gather facts about selling the item before you make your decision about whether to keep or sell it.

9

I'll Think about It Tomorrow

SOMETIMES WE think that if we only had more money everything would be fine. If we were wealthy, all our problems would be solved. The truth is, having a lot of money does not absolve people from taking financial responsibility. We all have to learn and use financial basics. Just look at the number of big lottery winners who amazingly run through their money in a couple of years. Kyle learned these lessons after she went to college.

KYLE'S STORY

I went to college with a generous allowance. My parents paid my tuition and room and board—everything. Later on, I got my own apartment and had to pay rent, utilities, and other household expenses, but my parents increased my allowance to cover those costs. You would think I had it made, but I'm a put-it-off kind of girl. I focused entirely on school and my social life and didn't pay much attention to my finances. I didn't open my bills. I threw them into a file box. I said I'd get to them later, but I never found the time.

But not taking care of my money preyed on my mind. *I woke up at* *night worrying about bills, promising myself that first thing in the morning I'd get everything organized and write checks.*

Morning would come, I'd go to class and forget about my bills until the next night. Three months passed; everything came to a head when the telephone company turned off my service, and my dad couldn't get hold of me at my apartment. He called me on my cell phone to tell me that my phone had been disconnected. I hadn't even noticed!

Dad was furious and got the whole story out of me in short order. I can't hold out on my dad. He told me to come home that weekend and bring all my bills with me.

We sat at the breakfast table. He told me to open all the envelopes, organize the bills by name, with the latest one on top. It took a while. I sat quietly while he looked at each pile. Then he turned to me and yelled that I had probably ruined my credit rating. He was disappointed in me; he thought I was more responsible.

My mom came in, thank goodness, and she took over while my dad cooled off. I got another lecture about being responsible. She got my attention.

She said, "Kyle, you've always procrastinated—we've talked about this before. You put things off until later. But you've never had to manage your finances before and now this behavior is affecting your life more significantly. You can choose to go through life this way and believe me, it's your choice, or you can make changes. It's up to you. Think about the way you want to live your life. Do you want to live fully and in the moment or do you want to drift—thinking about accomplishment but delaying your action? You won't achieve nearly as much that way which is not what I want for you, but it's your choice. You decide."

My parents hadn't talked to me in such a strong way before. *I shaped up for a while—opening and paying my bills on time, but then I slid back into my old habits. I was too busy and thought that I'd take care of the bills later. But my mother's harsh words about my procrastination worried me. She was right. And it hurt that she felt that way about me. I realized I not only put off paying bills, but I put off a lot of things.*

I didn't return phone calls promptly and sometimes not at all. Class reading assignments were done just before the test or quiz. Term papers were completed in a panic at the last moment and often turned in late. I avoided meeting with my counselor to discuss my future career plans.

I began to grasp what my mom meant by living life fully. If I didn't jump in, get things done, I would sit around thinking about doing them. And that meant I never moved on to other things. I was letting the little tasks of living paralyze me.

I had to change. *It didn't happen overnight. Even though I have been working on not procrastinating for several years, I still have this tendency to put things off. But I have learned to handle it. For example, I open all my mail every day and I pay my bills as soon as I receive them. I know I might earn a few cents in interest if I paid them when they're due, but it works better for me to write a check as soon as I open the bill. That way, bill paying isn't such a big job and it helps make me feel on top of things. Anytime I can get the payment automatically deducted from my checking account, I arrange that.*

As far as term papers and reading assignments went, I developed a "head start" regimen on projects. I started to read textbooks before classes began so that I stayed ahead of the assignments. I felt more confident in my studies, learned more, and enjoyed my classes. My grades improved too. Term papers were complex for me to figure out how to get them finished on schedule, so I started on the paper as soon as I got the assignment and set aside time every day to work on it. My energy level stayed up when I made steady progress on the assignment. Most of all, I was filled with a sense of success when I finished it on time.

Now that I'm in the work world, these same techniques help me get proposals and reports together in a timely fashion. These methods may sound simplistic, but since I've never figured out why I procrastinate I can only find ways to circumvent the tendency. I haven't solved all my problems, but the more I create systematic ways of doing things, the better I deal with this trait.

Besides paying my bills on time, *I learned to balance my checkbook every month. I know some people say that's not necessary anymore since banking is computerized and there is little chance of a bank error. That's what I tried to tell my dad. He said that banks may not make many mistakes, but we do. He asked me how I knew how much money I had in checking if I didn't balance my account? I retorted that I used the ATM to get my current balance. He sighed and said that was not my true balance.*

But I discovered another reason to balance my checking account. I don't spend hours doing it. In fact, it only takes me about fifteen or twenty minutes a month. What it does is help me review the past month, look at how I spent my money, and think about my future money issues. Do I want to buy a piece of furniture, add to my retirement account, or go on vacation this winter? The act of sitting at my desk balancing my checkbook centers me around my money—gives me a sense of control.

For a while, I also matched up my credit card receipts with the listing on the statement, but I decided that was too much work. Now I read through the list of charges and if something looks off or I don't remember it, I check my folding file for the receipt or I call the credit card company for more information.

I've never had an incorrect billing on my credit card bill, but I have seen things I wasn't expecting. One time I was out of town for a couple weeks and mailed my credit card payment on the payment deadline. They charged me a $29 late fee. I called the credit card company and they removed the charge for that one time but cautioned me to send the payment on time in the future.

I didn't realize I was paying a $60 annual fee after the first year for my credit card. That charge showed up on the statement at the end of twelve months. The information about the annual fee was buried in the application form I signed for the card, which I didn't read carefully. I decided to keep the card—I collect air miles for every dollar I charge—but now I want to know what I'm paying for. Before, anything could show up on my credit card, and I would have paid it.

I wish I had started managing my finances before college. *If so, I might not have gotten so out of control my first time away from home. Once I focused on my issues of procrastination with money and changed my behavior regarding finances, I applied the same principles to other areas of my life. I developed better relationships with friends. I became more assertive. I didn't waste time. My grades improved. I met with a counselor and set my career path in motion. And I proved to myself and my parents that I could take control of my life.*

PROCRASTINATION

It is so easy to put off financial matters. Getting down to paying bills each month is difficult for a lot of people. Some of my clients describe getting cold sweats or feeling dread at the prospect of writing all those checks. It might also stem from the reluctance to give up that cash sitting in checking. At any rate, you cannot afford to delay paying your bills. You need to find ways to make it less painful and more automatic. Kyle's idea of paying a bill as soon as it arrives in the mail makes sense if you have the money in checking. That way, you are usually only writing one check; it's quicker and takes barely any of your time. If you are living paycheck to paycheck, pay bills every time you receive your pay.

Your bank may offer bill-paying options using your personal computer. Certain businesses will agree to automatically deduct the monthly payment directly from your checking account. Automatic deductions are handy for those fixed monthly payments like rent, insurance, or a car payment. You may enjoy using a software program that will write checks for you. You can even download your bank account data and automatically balance your bank account. Some of these methods will make the bill-paying process and bank reconciliation go a little easier for you.

OPEN YOUR MAIL

Kyle said she didn't open her mail regularly. Opening your mail is the first step to taking responsibility for your financial life.

While interviewing people about what they had learned about money, a recent graduate proudly told me he had finally paid off all his credit card debt in three years after graduation. But then he got a big surprise. Damien said he never bothered to open the monthly bank statements or balance his checking account. One day he got a phone call from a clerk at a local bookstore telling him his check was returned for insufficient funds. Puzzled, he quickly looked at his bank statements and was shocked to discover that he had been overdrafting his account regularly. He had overdraft protection for his checking account, but Damien had exceeded the credit limit on the overdraft account.

OVERDRAFT PROTECTION

If you request overdraft protection, the bank will cover overdrafts by charging an account set up for this purpose. The bank establishes a line of credit based on your request—maybe $200 to $1,000. Any overdrafts in checking are funded by this account. Information about any overdrafts appear on the monthly bank statement along with a request to pay at least a minimum amount on the overdraft account, just like a credit card. If the client doesn't pay, the bank automatically deducts the payment from checking and charges interest on the unpaid balance. Damien was building another high interest debt, and he didn't even know it! This is another good reason to open your mail and to balance your checkbook every month.

Overdraft protection is a safety net. We all make mistakes from time to time—forgetting to enter a check or an ATM withdrawal. With overdraft protection, you can be assured of avoiding expensive charges for bad checks. Make a promise to yourself that you will always pay off any charges to your overdraft account in the month you receive your bank statement. If you treat this service like a credit card where you carry a balance owed, you risk exceeding your limit, and the bank will not cover your check. A returned check is embarrassing and expensive. The bank will charge a fee, and many creditors also charge for a bounced check. You could end up paying $40 to $50 for one bad check, not to mention the time you will spend getting everything straightened out.

MORE THAN MONEY

Kyle discovered something significant—a sense of order in one's life and taking charge. The tendency to delay doing the things in life that must be done depletes energy. If you take charge of your financial life, you will find that other parts of your existence will improve too. For many people, the art of maintaining a systematic financial life seems too hard, so they don't bother. As a result, other parts of their existence take on disorder too. Kyle found simple ways to stay on top of her finances, and in doing so she was rewarded in many ways. Her approach to schoolwork changed, and her grades improved. Her friends no longer perceived her as flaky or irresponsible. Oftentimes we think change requires massive, groundbreaking steps. But Kyle made small, simple changes to improve. You can too.

FINANCIAL BASICS

- Open your mail in a timely fashion.
- Pay your bills on time, or if you tend to procrastinate pay them when you receive the bill.
- Check out automatic bill paying or online banking if this system works for you.
- Be sure to have overdraft protection for your checking account.

10

Now Where Did I Put That?

DO YOU HAVE a formal filing system for important papers? Do you secure your blank checks, credit card, and bank statements in a safe place? You probably have an informal system for such things. Tim had his own system and he thought he had his paperwork under control until he almost missed a semester of classes.

TIM'S STORY

I've always used the "pile" system. At any one time I have four to six piles of papers on my desk. One pile for coming events and concerts, one for class assignments, one or more piles for term papers I am working on, one for all the graduate school information I am collecting, one for my bills and other financial stuff. You get the idea. This system always worked well for me when I was at home. When I went to college, I didn't give any thought to changing my system. Boy, was I wrong! I got seriously messed up and messed with because of my sloppy methods.

I remember bragging to my new roommates *that my system worked and that I always knew where everything was. Of course, my desk looked like a disaster, but I was on top of things. I have a good memory and could* always remember which pile I put something in. Just to be sure though, every once in a while, I'd go through one of my piles to refresh my memory about what was there and restack the papers in a neat pile.

This method was working pretty well at college, until one warm autumn day my roommate Chuck needed fresh air, opened all the windows, then left for class. A wind gusted through the room. It took hours to pick up all the papers and sort them out again. My roommates thought it was hilarious and kidded me about my system. I decided to "secure" my files by collecting heavy rocks I set on top of each pile of papers.

Life went on. I was happy to be in college, enjoyed my classes, and had a good social life. My roommates and I had a lot of friends who dropped into our room. Our dorm was a happening place, and I liked the action even if I didn't always know the visitors.

All my financial stuff was in one pile: student loan information, credit card and telephone numbers in case I lost one and had to report it, PINs, bank statements, checkbook, a box of blank checks, paid and unpaid bills, and a debit card that I didn't use very often.

My parents paid for my tuition and half the room and board. They wanted me to begin to learn how to manage my money, so they made a monthly deposit into my checking account, a portion of the money I needed for the year. It was up to me to make sure I kept track of what I would need to pay next semester's expenses and tuition, and set aside part of the funds for these future bills. I was good at this. I never was a big spender and didn't feel tempted to spend all my cash. I made a note in my checkbook every month about how much money I was saving for next semester, and I didn't add that amount into the balance that I was using on a day-to-day basis.

As classes got more demanding, I got busier. I quit balancing my checkbook. It wasn't a big deal. I knew I wouldn't bounce any checks because I had quite a bit of money in checking. I planned to balance the account between semesters.

Just before I went home for break, I wrote checks to the university for the next semester's tuition and dorm fees. I still hadn't balanced my checkbook, but I wasn't concerned. I was sure there was enough money to cover the checks.

After I'd been home for a week, I got a notice from the university that my checks had been returned for insufficient funds. I would be denied admission for the next semester. I was in shock. There had to be some mistake—a screw-up by the bank. I called the bank, and they told me I had $1,200 in checking. I thought I had over $10,000! The banker suggested I review my statements. Perhaps a deposit was not made or I made an error in addition.

I started balancing my checking account with the bank statements. September checked out fine. All the October deposits were there, just as my parents had promised. The funny thing was that under the section listing checks I had written was a check number that was way out of sequence. I had been writing checks starting with 200. This check was number 322 and it was for a large amount—$2,200. I thought maybe the bank charged someone else's check against my account. In November and December, the same thing happened. Three more checks appeared out of sequence—323, 324, and 325 all written for $2,200 each. A total of $8,800 had been deducted from my checking account. Checks I had not written!

I immediately called the bank. When I told them I had not written the four checks, they said they would order a copy of each check and send it to me. I told them I didn't have much time—if I didn't get this straightened out, I wouldn't be able to return to school. They said they would put a rush on it.

In the meantime, I called the Fee Collection office and talked with the manager. I explained the situation and asked her if there was anything I could do. She said she would make a note in my file, but I needed to get my fees paid in full, plus pay late-fee penalties by Monday or I wouldn't be admitted for next term. She suggested I have the bank wire the money to the Fee Collection office or pay over the phone with a credit card. I didn't have a big enough credit line to handle the fees, and I told her I would get back to her.

I decided I'd better tell my parents what was going on. They said they would pay my fees with their credit card, if I would agree to review my banking information with them.

The copies of the four checks came two days later. They looked like my checks. My name was signed on the signature line, but it was not my signature. I couldn't figure out what had happened, until my dad asked me where I kept my blank checks. I told him they were in my financial pile. He asked if this pile was locked in a desk. I told him the story about the heavy rock on the top of the pile.

He explained stolen blank checks. Someone had opened the box of blank checks on top of my desk, stolen checks, and forged my signature. Oftentimes the thief takes checks from the back of the book so the loss won't be noticed right away. Dad thought we would be able to get the money back from the bank—they could only honor my signature—but we'd better notify them immediately.

The bank said they would compare the signature on the forged checks to the signature card I signed when I opened the account. In the meantime, they told me to report the theft to the campus police. The police officer said she would file a report, and when I returned to campus I should come to their office to make a complete statement.

I couldn't believe one of my roommates would forge checks. Dad said if I left my blank checks out in plain view, anyone could be tempted. I told him that we had a lot of visitors, some of them strangers to me. It was time for me to lock my checks in the desk.

Dad said he thought I'd better rethink my "pile" system too. *Not just checks. Certain items need to be protected such as PINs, social security number, credit and debit cards, and bank statements. Everything must be locked in a safe place.*

I got everything straightened out with the bank and the university, and I returned to class for the next term. The police investigated, but they never caught anyone. They published a notice in the student newspaper warning other students of the potential problem. I was glad. I had never heard of such a thing—stolen blank checks and forged signatures on a college campus. If I had known, I might have been more careful. I felt fortunate. Things got settled without too much financial loss to me. And no one stole my credit card, social security card, or my identity.

I still operate on a pile system, but all my financial and personal information gets locked up every day. I just transferred the financial piles to my desk drawer.

PROTECTING SENSITIVE MATERIALS

Your dorm room is not the most private or secure place you could live, so you need to exercise a little more care in protecting your financial assets from theft or inquisitive people.

Blank checks are sensitive documents and need to be treated as if they were cash. Tim's story highlights one of the reasons why checking accounts need to be balanced every month. He would have caught the problem months earlier and saved a lot of anxious moments and time.

This story of stolen checks also points out why we keep a check register listed with consecutive check numbers as we write checks. If you notice a missing check number in your register, call your bank or access your account online to see if the check has cleared your account. You may have written a check and neglected to record it. Ask the bank for the name of the payee and the amount. If you have written the check, this information will probably jog your memory. If you are sure you have not written the check, notify the bank immediately. If the check has not cleared the bank, you can stop payment on the check so that it will not be charged against your account. There will probably be a fee for this service. If the check has already cleared, pull the check from your bank statement, or if your bank does not return checks ask the bank to send a copy.

TAKE ACTION

Always notify the appropriate people and organizations. Tim called the bank and the university. He notified the police in the jurisdiction where the theft took place. Then he asked his parents for help. This is not the time to put things off and hope everything will work out. You need to attack the issue and get it straightened out. If you do not know what to do, ask someone you trust to help or check with the appropriate officials at the university.

Sometimes the little things in life defeat us. Tim was proud of his pile system, but it had its drawbacks: spending precious time sifting through piles of paper looking for a particular item, turning a room upside down looking for an important article needed for a paper, and forgetting to pay a bill because it's in the wrong pile or slipped in between the pages of a magazine. Not only do we lose time and get discouraged, we can adversely affect our credit history by not having a system.

To some people, the words "having a system" seem like too

much work. You can create a simple but efficient method as you start your financial life. Simple systems enable you to save time, energy, and negative emotions. Secure, organized files allow you to rest a little easier knowing your financial information is protected.

WHAT DOCUMENTS SHOULD BE SAVED

The following list will guide you on what to save and for how long:

- Your birth certificate, social security card, passport, marriage license, and divorce papers. Keep these forever.
- Tax returns. Keep the filled-out forms, W-2 and 1099 forms in a permanent file. Any supporting documentation (you probably will not have any as a student) can be thrown out after three years. Keep supporting documents for seven years if you have a more complicated return.
- Student loan agreements, student financial aid notices, statements, and correspondence. Keep for the life of the loan.
- Other loan agreements and lease contracts such as for an automobile. Keep for the life of the lease.
- Credit card paperwork that includes the card number and a toll-free number to call in case it is lost or stolen. This information usually is sent with the credit card. Keep for as long as you have the credit card.
- Credit card statements. Keep for one year.
- Bank statements for checking and savings accounts, and canceled checks (if your bank returns them to you). Keep for one year.
- Receipts for important items. Keep for one year except for items under warranty.
- Warranties for your computer or other items covered. Keep for the life of the warranty.
- Insurance policies. Keep as long as the policy is active.

STORAGE OPTIONS

That's a formidable list at first glance. What is the best way to keep this information? There are several ways to handle this. You could buy a small filing cabinet or a cardboard file and designate folders for all these items. If you enjoy keeping records in this way, go ahead. But as a college student, you will not have a huge amount of information to keep on file, so an easy way to keep it all in one place is to buy a large three-ring binder and plastic envelope inserts. As you receive documents that need to be saved, slide them in the plastic envelopes. This way, you can leaf through your notebook and quickly retrieve what you are looking for. This works particularly well for loan documents, insurance policies, birth certificate, passport, and so on—papers you will be keeping for a while or forever. You may want to keep everything in this file or you may decide that bank statements, credit card statements, and receipts—items you will throw out in a year or so—can go in an expanding file. You can throw them away at the end of a year and reuse the file.

If you are concerned about the security of certain permanent documents, rent a safe-deposit box at your bank. Or you may want to keep them in a fire-resistant lockbox.

If you are using a personal accounting software package, be sure to back up your data regularly. It is time consuming to re-create a financial history.

Whatever system you use, make sure it is secure—that it can be locked up. A desk drawer with a lock is fine if you are using the binder system. And be sure to lock up your blank checks and information on your PINs.

Consider giving your parents a list of your vital information so they have a back-up copy in case of an emergency.

IDENTITY THEFT

There is growing concern about identity theft. Never give your social security number unless there is a good reason for using it, like on your tax return or bank account application. Do not use your social security card as identification.

When you throw away credit card receipts or statements make sure your account number is obliterated by inking out the number, tearing the receipt, or shredding these papers. While some merchants' receipts obscure all but the last four account numbers, many receipts still list the full credit card number. Unscrupulous people have been known to go through trash looking for active credit card numbers.

If your wallet is lost or stolen, notify your bank and credit card companies of debit and credit card losses. Go one step further. Notify the three national credit-reporting organizations to place a fraud alert on your name and social security number:

1. Equifax (888) 766–0008; www.equifax.com
2. Experian (888) 397–3742; www.experian.com
3. TransUnion (800) 888–4213; www.tuc.com

It is a good idea to order a credit report annually. This will show if someone has opened a charge or credit card account using your name without your knowledge. There have been instances where accounts have been opened with a new mailing address so that the responsible person is not aware of charges building in their name. The monthly bill never reaches the responsible party and the identity thieves go their merry way.

CREATE A SYSTEM FOR YOUR FINANCIAL LIFE

Find a way to keep all your unpaid bills in a place where you won't lose or forget them. You can use a file envelope or a desk drawer where only unpaid bills are kept. One way to be sure you haven't missed a payment is to pay the bill as soon as it arrives. If you can create a system for your financial life, one that you can consistently follow, you will be rewarded with extra time and the peace of mind that comes with an orderly life.

FINANCIAL BASICS

- Keep important information in safe and secure places.
- Develop a simple system to pay bills and for storage of all vital information.
- Always sign your checks the same as the bank signature card you signed when you opened your account.
- Never give out your credit card number or social security number over the phone to a stranger who calls you.
- If you notice a discrepancy on any financial statements, or if something is lost or stolen, immediately notify your banking institution.

11

What's Next?

YOU HAVE YOUR degree, you found a good job, and now you will be receiving a regular salary. You also have a lot of pent-up desire for possessions. You deferred many purchases for the past few years, and now with the prospect of more money coming in every month it is tempting to go out and buy everything you believe you will need as you enter a new phase of your life. This is another time to pause, take stock, and think about your financial future. Todd's brother helped him plan his entry into the working world.

TODD'S STORY

What a relief! I was finally done with college and had a great job lined up. I even got a signing bonus with my new company. My starting salary with the real estate investment firm was $50,000 with the possibility of a year-end bonus, and I got $10,000 up front. I didn't even have to move to another town. I was feeling very prosperous until my older brother, Roth, had a chat with me.

He warned me *not to make the same mistakes he made. He never told anyone about his problems because he was so embarrassed. He confided in me because he thought it might save me from financial hardship.*

Roth felt on top of the world when he graduated from college. He had some student loans and had been careful not to accumulate credit card debt, but when he graduated, he felt rich, quickly bought a new car, found a great apartment, hired a decorator to furnish it, and purchased expensive clothes. A bright future ahead, he thought he needed to look the part. He was ready to take on the world.

With his new salary, he could easily manage, so he bought everything he wanted. Monthly cell phone, premium cable, DSL line, and health club bills left him without extra spending money. Lunches, a new laptop computer, and an electronic planner further drained his pocket. Every month he saw something else he thought he should have for business or pleasure.

Roth neglected to keep track of his monthly payments, plus all his other monthly living expenses. He had a rough idea, but he was matching his expenses against his gross salary. He forgot about insurance and payroll taxes that would be withheld from his check. Reality surfaced when he got his first paycheck. His take-home pay was a third lower than he expected.

Roth had to backpedal fast in order to stay afloat financially. He returned clothes, stopped the decorator in mid-job, sold the new car at a loss and got a used one. Even so, he racked up $20,000 in credit card debt that would take a couple of years to pay off. He no longer enjoyed all the things he had accumulated. Money worries plagued him.

Roth offered to help me work out a financial plan for my first year. After hearing his story, I knew I'd be a fool not to take advantage of his knowledge.

The first thing we did was ask the human resources office of my new company to determine my take-home pay amount from the monthly salary and the signing bonus. Knowing my monthly cash income helped settle me into my financial status as a young professional.

Roth asked me to make a wish list of everything I wanted *to buy. That was awesome. I wanted a sports car, a bigger apartment, new living room furniture, a European vacation, a skiing trip to Aspen, and a big-screen TV. I knew I couldn't afford it, but it was fun fantasizing. I estimated the cost of each item on my wish list.*

Roth told me to write each item on 3x5 index cards, look them over the next few weeks, put them in priority order, and make up new cards for any other things that came to mind. I prioritized and then reprioritized the wish-list cards. The cards helped me think about what was most important to me. Since I was also preparing a list of all my basic living expenses at the same time, I began to think about alternatives to my expensive items. Were there things on the wish list I wanted that could be fulfilled in other ways? How long was I willing to wait for a particular item?

Two weeks later I had my prioritized list, my take-home pay, and my budget for basic expenses. Roth handed me a worksheet, and we filled in the blanks. My finances looked good, and I was still planning that skiing trip when Roth asked me if I had signed up for the company's 401(k) plan. I hadn't, thinking I would put it off for a while until I got settled financially. Roth persuaded me to sign up immediately.

The company matched my contributions *up to 3% of my salary. For every dollar I put in, the company put in another dollar. As Roth pointed out, this was like getting a raise my first month. He also told me the earlier I started putting away retirement money, the more likely it would be that I could retire when I wanted or change careers later on. It would give me a lot of freedom, and if I started paying in now I'd never miss the money. I wasn't so sure about that, but I trusted Roth's advice and signed up for the retirement plan.*

As we worked on the budget, I kept revising my wish list. I decided to stay in my apartment for at least another year. I liked the place, and the price was right. I put half the signing bonus into savings and spent the rest of the money on a nice leather armchair, a new TV, and a down payment for a used car.

It's been five years since I graduated from college. I'm so thankful I listened to my older brother. As time progressed, I received salary increases, built my savings and investments, and purchased other luxury items I wanted. I don't have any credit card debt. Roth saved me from a lot of sleepless nights worrying about money, and last year to pay him back I took him to Aspen with me.

LOOK TO THE FUTURE

The very first thing you do after accepting a new job is sign up for your organization's retirement program and put the maximum amount allowed into the plan. And promise yourself you will increase the contribution as you receive raises and qualify for a higher contribution. Don't worry about not having enough money to live on—you *will* adjust to your take-home pay. Remember you will be bringing in a lot more money than you had in college. If you have been careful not to accumulate any expensive credit card debt and kept your student loans in check, you will not have any trouble living on the new salary, minus the retirement contributions.

You may be tempted to wait to start your retirement planning. After all, you are young, you have many years before you will actually retire. Assume you want $1,000,000 when you are sixty-five. If you start saving at age eighteen, earning a 10% return, you need to save $78 a month. If you wait until you are twenty-five to start saving, you will need to put away $258 a month. At thirty-five, you will need $442 and at forty-five your savings will have to be $1,317 a month in order to reach your goal of $1,000,000 at age sixty-five. This example demonstrates the power of compound interest. The earlier you start saving, the less you will have to invest over time because your money is working for you, growing and adding to your retirement savings.

If your new employer does not have a retirement plan, go to your bank or a financial services company and ask them to set up an individual retirement account (IRA) or Roth IRA account for you.

The contribution to an IRA is deductible from taxable income, but the funds withdrawn at retirement are fully taxable. A Roth IRA contribution is not deductible from taxable income, but withdrawals at retirement are not taxed. Check your options. A Roth IRA, if you qualify, is probably most beneficial to you.

Every month, have the financial institution automatically transfer one-twelfth of the maximum amount you can contribute from your checking account into your new IRA account. I recommend investing in a good stock mutual fund when you are young because this money will be invested for many years, and experience has shown us that the stock market produces the best return over time.

COVER YOURSELF

You will need to make decisions on other benefits offered by your employer. In addition to signing up for medical insurance with your new organization, be sure to apply for disability insurance, even if you have to pay the premium yourself. Long-term disability insurance is especially important for the young, because if the unthinkable happens a person needs to have supplemental income that will last a lifetime. In other words, if you were paralyzed in an auto accident and unable to earn enough money to be independent, disability insurance could fill the gap, give you financial security, and reduce the stress of inadequate funds over your lifetime, which could be more than fifty years.

COST OF LIVING

Draw up a new spending plan. It will have two components: the monthly or regular costs to live—rent, insurance, utilities, food, student loan payments, renter's insurance, and the one-time costs for starting a new life. These one-time costs may include a deposit on a new apartment, moving expenses, a new wardrobe, a car down payment, furniture, outfitting a kitchen, and other household items. These costs can mount quickly and may seem overwhelming, but remember, knowledge is power. If you have this information down in writing where you can review it, you can make rational decisions before you sink into debt.

It will be to your benefit and long-term financial security to start out slowly on your spending when you begin your career. Give yourself some time to experience your new costs of living. Then adjust your plan as you learn more. It is very difficult to start spending more money than you can afford and try to cut back later. Some people rationalize the shortfall. They start borrowing on credit cards believing that they can make up the deficit after the next raise or bonus. That kind of thinking is a guaranteed path to a lifetime of debt.

MONTHLY SAVINGS AND EMERGENCY FUNDS

Remember to build in a monthly amount to be saved each month in your spending plan. This is in addition to your retirement contribution. Initially, allocate your savings to build an emergency fund of three to six months of living expenses. The purpose of the emergency fund is to give you financial security in the event you are not earning an income or you have some unexpected financial demands. This could happen if your company goes under or downsizes. Or you might be injured and need medical treatment not covered by insurance. Or you are required to relocate and your company does not fully cover the costs of moving.

Invest your emergency fund in a savings or money market account. You want to be able to access the cash immediately. After you are satisfied with the emergency fund, continue your savings program and allocate your funds to other longer-term investment vehicles such as Certificates of Deposit, Treasury bills, stocks, and bonds. Begin to educate yourself on investment strategies by reading or attending a class or lecture. Many financial institutions give free lectures on various financial topics and educational institutions offer classes through their continuing education divisions.

WISH-LIST CARDS

You may have more start-up costs than money as you start your new career. Before you take on debt to fund these costs, do what Todd did. Write down each potential purchase on an index card. Play with the cards for a few weeks; arrange them in the order of most importance to you. New ideas may come to mind as you review the cards. For example, you may decide to get along without a car for a year or buy a used car instead of a new one. Write down these new ideas on cards and see how those changes affect your thinking. But be honest with yourself. If a new car is of the utmost importance, then figure out how you can get it within your income. It may mean giving up other things and if you decide you can do that, go for it!

The 3x5 card method is also useful if you come into some unexpected money like an inheritance or cash prize. I used this method with a client who became a multimillionaire overnight when her firm was acquired. Her biggest fear was that she would fritter away this unexpected bonanza.

She spent several months playing with options like retiring, sending her niece and nephews to graduate school, or buying a jazz club. She ultimately decided to continue working for the new firm, bought some finery (her word for new clothes), reassured her aging mother that she would provide for her, and became a partner in a jazz club. She deliberately used 3x5 cards the color of green—not to symbolize money, but to represent life and growth. She said the cards gave her a good fix on what was important to her in the long run.

OTHER NEEDS FOR A NEW LIFE

Be sure you understand the prevailing dress climate in your work environment before you buy a new wardrobe. I remember a young professor starting her first teaching job at a prestigious university. She was advised that business suits were appropriate only to find out once she had purchased five new suits that none of the other professors dressed that way. She spent $3,000 on clothing that could have been used for other purposes.

One way to assemble a less expensive work wardrobe is to shop at resale shops that specialize in top quality clothing, or look for discount clothing through the Internet. After you have a basic wardrobe, you can shop sales to add other items.

If you need furniture, check with your relatives. Maybe someone has an attic full of things that you could borrow or use permanently. Look into buying used furniture by going to garage sales, auctions, or stores that handle used furniture. Perhaps you'll find a talent in refinishing pieces or learning how to reupholster a chair.

SOURCES OF FUNDS

Once you are certain of your immediate needs, what should you do if you still need extra money? Sometimes your firm will have a credit union. This may be your best source of money because credit unions usually offer slightly lower interest rates for car loans and personal loans to their members. However, you may have to be a member of the credit union for a certain number of months before taking out a loan. If a credit union loan is not possible, go to your bank and talk with them about getting a loan. Try not to fund your start-up costs using your credit card. It is just too expensive.

Perhaps your parents or grandparents would be willing to loan you money at the current bank rate. Draw up a simple contract with them stating:

1. amount borrowed
2. interest rate
3. amount you will pay each month on the loan date of the monthly payment

You can create an amortization schedule for the loan by using a financial calculator or going to a Web site that has a calculator (visit www.bankrate.com). Hold to that repayment schedule. You want to have a good credit rating with your relatives. You never know when you may need help in the future, and they will be more likely to advance you money if you have shown your good intentions about repayment. On the other hand, if you think asking relatives for a loan will create tension in the family, don't do it. Look for other sources of funds. It is not worth the strain.

You will know how much you can afford to repay on a loan because you have already drawn up a spending plan. Be sure to keep your total monthly loan payments, including student loans, at no more than 10 to 15 percent of your monthly take-home pay. If you find your monthly debt repayment approaching 20 percent, take steps to reduce your loans by cutting other expenses and paying more each month on your debt.

RETURN TO YOUR SPENDING PLAN

Monitor your expenses carefully during the first three or four months of your new professional life to see if your spending plan is on target. It is almost impossible to draw up an exact list of monthly expenditures, so you will be fine-tuning your plan as you go along. Some people like to consistently monitor their spending and keep detailed records. There are good software packages available to track finances, such as Microsoft Money or Quicken, or a spreadsheet can be designed to accomplish the same thing.

You need to find your best way to manage your money. Not everyone manages money in the same way, but we all have to take responsibility for our financial life. The key to mastering your money is to find what works for you while staying within certain financial boundaries:

1. paying bills on time
2. keeping debt within reason
3. saving for the future

Not only do we not all manage finances the same way, we do not all *spend* money the same way. Pay attention to what is important to you and what is not. I have four children. One son buys fresh flowers every week for his home. He and his wife enjoy them, and they say it brings them pleasure. My daughter would never spend money on cut flowers. She considers that an extravagance and buys plants that don't have to be replaced. She would rather spend her money on books. My son uses the public library for reading material. But each one is right. They both knowingly make their decisions within their financial parameters.

This diversity in spending is important to remember as you bring a life partner into your world. You want to give each other some financial freedom as you learn to live together so that one can buy fresh flowers every week and the other books. This may mean keeping your money separate and funding the common expenses by setting up a third checking account that you both contribute to based on your income. Another way to add freedom for individual needs is for each partner to have their own "kitty" that they can spend in any way they wish.

As you pay attention to your spending habits and desires, you will begin to figure out your financial nature. The important thing is for you to knowingly make your choices. Be flexible and make changes when necessary. Live fully in the present but remain aware of the future. Master your finances today while at the same time saving and preparing for a secure future.

FINANCIAL BASICS

- After you graduate from college and land a permanent job, carefully look at your salary and figure out your take-home pay (after taxes and other deductions).
- Be sure to sign up for a retirement plan and medical and disability insurance.
- Create a spending plan for your new life. This will help you decide on what you can afford to purchase immediately, and what items will have to be deferred.
- Develop a savings and emergency fund category in your spending plan.

12

Develop a Personal Philosophy of Money

AS YOU WORK your way through *Financial Basics,* be aware of those money management techniques that appeal to you. They will help you begin to develop your personal philosophy of money—fundamental principles that you can rely on to guide you through your financial life.

In this chapter we will explore some examples of some financial ways of thinking—ideas you may want to adopt as your own.

GIVE THANKS

Karen used to dread bill paying. She hated writing checks that reduced her bank account balance. One morning while having coffee with her friend, Laurel described a way of giving thanks that was meaningful to her. Karen listened, was intrigued, and that evening wrote a list of all the things in life she was grateful for. She discovered that listing her blessings rather than dwelling on misfortune, highlighting positive aspects of life rather than perceived failures, elevated her mood and gave her a sense of peace. She initiated the practice of giving thanks each day for the good things in her life.

This daily exercise found its way into her financial life. As she fearfully approached her desk to pay her monthly bills, she suddenly remembered the lesson of gratitude and decided to apply the concept to bill paying. While writing each check Karen thinks of benefits received: electricity/light, gas/warmth, and car payment/reliable transportation. She gives thanks for these things and sends each check in the mail with gratitude that she has the resources to pay. She does not begrudge her creditors and lament her declining bank balance. Instead of holding tight to her money, she gladly pays her bills. This does not mean that she is a spendthrift. Far from it. She practices good financial management, and she trusts that abundance will circulate back to her.

Karen no longer hates to pay her bills, and she is convinced her new attitude of thankfulness creates a positive energy around her money. She believes she is more prosperous today, and it is partially due to her new attitude toward money. Karen especially appreciates the feeling of ease she now has with money.

SHARE

Young people are generous and giving. Students are interested in volunteer activities and commit time to worthy projects. A recent news article featured a group of students who spent their spring break building houses for Habitat for Humanity—a splendid gesture of giving something of yourself to another.

A vice president for finance at a small private college counsels graduating students to "give five." She suggests that after getting a full-time job, graduates give 5 percent of their monthly take-home pay to charitable and arts organizations that are doing work they believe is important.

She goes on to advise new graduates to give five hours a month as a volunteer to an organization where they can make a difference. She believes "giving five" will enhance the graduate's life as well as the community around him.

Marie loves to tell how she began to share. Her mother had instilled the concept of philanthropy when she was a child, telling Marie that she would see a benefit if she shared part of her money.

When Marie started her new career, she gave money to charitable organizations and sat back waiting for money to flow back to her. Nothing happened.

Chagrined, she challenged her mother on the philosophy of sharing. Her mother smiled and told her the most important part of sharing was to do it freely, without thoughts of rewards. Marie, trusting her mother, donated money again. This time she chose organizations she believed were doing important work. She contributed to a shelter for battered women and a local ballet company.

As she wrote her monthly checks, she wished the organizations well. She imagined a new blanket for a woman in the shelter and the next performance of *Swan Lake,* a tradition she and her mother, once a ballerina, shared. After three years of sending donations, she began to volunteer with the ballet company, working on set designs, then agreed to serve on their board. During her first board meeting, she met the love of her life.

Marie says it's all about cause and effect. If you open up a door, one thing leads to the next. And, in the end, she believes she gained more from her contributions than the organizations that received her time and money.

BE MELLOW WITH MONEY

Money issues are emotionally charged for many people. It is easy to let worry and fear pervade the consciousness and assume a prominent place in life. Some people deal with these emotions by being contemptuous about money matters. Money is a dirty word to them, and they are proud they don't waste time balancing their bank account or funding their retirement plan. Deep down, though, they invest a lot of energy worrying about money. They haven't solved their money issues, only buried them.

Others are frightened of money. Sometimes they can't even articulate their fear. They only know money makes them nervous, and they would rather not think about their finances. But, of course, they do think about it. Their fear doesn't leave.

Some people believe it is too hard to keep track of money. They think they lack the ability to manage their finances and do the minimum amount to get by.

The only answer to these money fears and worries is to take control. Instead of letting money have power over you, dispel money emotions and anxiety by taking responsibility. Taking responsibility means paying bills on time, balancing the checkbook, spending within one's means, and saving part of income. This need not take a huge amount of your time. Use the suggestions throughout *Financial Basics.* Establish a weekly routine to deal with finances—set aside an hour during a quiet time of the week, maybe Sunday afternoon. Find your own best way to manage your money—a way that allows you to be mellow with money.

When working with clients who had difficulty managing their money, I was always surprised and pleased to see that those people who clearly wanted to become better money handlers did so. This was especially true of women who came to me saying they really didn't understand personal finances; they were afraid. I invariably found when the client was sincere about improving, she quickly learned how to take charge. Understanding basics about finances gave her the confidence to improve. Imparting fundamental knowledge resulting in personal financial empowerment is the goal of *Financial Basics.* With knowledge, you *can* overcome your fears. With practice, over time you *can* become a mellow and a better money manger.

FEEL PROSPEROUS

Jarrett realized he was investing a lot of emotional energy in money. He worried about money, wanted more money, and dreamed about the things he could buy if he had enough money. Money consumed his mind. He thought he would never have enough to live in the manner he desired. Over time he came to understand that if he were responsible with his money, not parsimonious, but spent within his means; if he stopped worrying whether he had enough, but trusted there would be resources available, he would have plenty.

Now, Jarrett believes if he feels prosperous, he will be prosperous.

He says if he allows breathing space in his life around money—and that means having a little extra put aside and not worrying if he has enough—he has more than enough.

Jarrett still loves and acquires beautiful things, but now he does it in a relaxed, fun way. He spends money within his resources, he saves money, and he does not invest emotional energy in worrying about money.

While exploring Jarrett's philosophy, the phrase *nest egg* came to mind. It's a comforting phrase, and if you have a nest egg you will feel more protected. Clients tell me if they have money put aside that is not earmarked and just there for security, they, paradoxically, seem to spend less. The compulsion to spend is gone. They feel more centered around money. But if they don't have a safety net, they feel nervous and fiscally stretched. At these times of money tension, they tend to buy, usually on credit, to buoy themselves with possessions. The feelings of lacking and associated compulsive spending disappear when they feel prosperous by having a nest egg. They don't deny themselves, they enjoy possessions that are important to them, but they don't give themselves what they don't need just to satisfy wild, out-of-control feelings that pop up when they are feeling financially lacking.

Establish your nest egg. It doesn't need to be large—maybe $50 to $250 to start. Tuck it in your desk drawer in an envelope that says NEST EGG in big letters or set up a special savings account at your bank. You may want to add to your nest egg as time goes on. Enjoy your special cache of funds. Notice your feelings around money. When you pay your bills, reflect on your finances over the last few weeks. Has your spending behavior changed in any way? Try feeling prosperous for six months and watch how it affects the rest of your life.

$ $ $

When you develop a personal philosophy of money, you begin to understand yourself and you take charge. You can give thanks for what you have, or share your money with the community, or become mellow with money by examining your fears, or you can practice feeling prosperous, therefore you become prosperous. Remember, it is about developing a unique philosophy of money that enables you to incorporate basic money management princi- ples in your everyday life. Whatever you choose to adopt for your- self, think of it as a positive affirmation toward your desired goals.

13

Your Story

YOU HAVE READ students' stories and reflected on the money management lessons they learned when they went to college. Now it is time to write your own story. Your story will give you the opportunity to identify your strong financial practices and name those areas you want to improve.

Our attitudes about money start early and are usually learned from those closest to us. Begin by examining the attitudes about money by those who raised you.

MY MOTHER OR FEMALE INFLUENCE

Complete the following sentences. Write as much as you need to fully explain.

- **My mother's attitude toward money is :**

_____

_____

_____

_____

- My mother manages money by:

_____
_____
_____
_____

- Concerning money, my mother always told me:

_____
_____
_____
_____

MY FATHER OR MALE INFLUENCE

- My father's attitude toward money is:

_____
_____
_____
_____

- My father manages money by:

_____
_____
_____
_____

- Concerning money, my father always told me:

_____
_____
_____
_____

You may be surprised at what you discover about your family's financial practices. It could be a positive recognition of good money handling, or you might realize that one or more of the adults in your life are still learning how to manage their finances. Now is the time to decide if you will emulate these influences or find a better way to manage your money.

Our peers and siblings provide additional influence in our lives and their attitudes about money will help you discover your own beliefs. Complete the following sentences to further delve into your influences.

- **My best friend handles his/her money by:**

  _____
  _____
  _____
  _____
  _____

- **My sibling handles money by:**

  _____
  _____
  _____
  _____
  _____

- **I disapprove of the way _____ handles his/her money because:**

  _____
  _____
  _____
  _____
  _____

Carefully review your responses to these statements, especially the last one. Sometimes, we reflect our own behavior when viewing others critically. If you don't approve of someone's money handling, there may be some components of that disapproval that are present in your actions. Think carefully about how you react to your negative feelings about other's financial behavior. Do you react negatively to another's financial activities because it mirrors your own?

Handling money effectively is a skill that requires thoughtfulness, awareness, knowledge, and experience. Is there someone you know who serves as a role model? A parent, friend, neighbor, teacher, employer, well-known businessperson, or perhaps a media or published spokesperson? Someone you believe possesses mastery over his or her finances? Take this time to write a sentence about your role model's successful money management techniques.

- **I think _____ successfully manages his/her finances because:**

  _____
  _____
  _____
  _____

Now answer the following questions about your own money management process. Use these questions and answers as catalysts to examine your attitudes.

- **I had an allowance as a child, and I usually spent it this way:**

  _____
  _____
  _____

- **I _____ saved part of my allowance, earnings, and cash gifts.**

  a. always
  b. never
  c. sometimes

- **I control my spending by**

  a. paying cash
  b. returning my purchases
  c. putting merchandise on hold to think it over
  d. I spend what I want

- **I _____ pay my bills on time.**

  a. always
  b. usually
  c. rarely

- **I have a savings account.**

  a. yes
  b. no

- **I balance my checkbook every month.**

  a. yes
  b. no

- **I have _____ credit card(s).**

- **I pay _____ on my credit card each month.**

  a. the balance due
  b. the minimum payment
  c. whatever I can afford

- **I don't have to worry about money—someone will bail me out if I get into trouble.**

  a. yes
  b. no
  c. maybe

- I don't worry about money—I will pay my debts when I graduate from college and start earning a salary.

  a. yes
  b. no

- I want to start my professional life with as little debt as possible, so I am careful not to spend more than necessary.

  a. yes
  b. no

- When it comes to money, I am afraid that

  _____
  _____
  _____
  _____
  _____

Using the information generated from the above exercises, make a list of your money strengths and weaknesses. Write these qualities quickly. Keep the pen moving. Don't edit yourself; you are looking for as big a list as possible. Write down everything you can think of.

STRENGTHS	WEAKNESSES

Take each strength on your list, write it again, and compliment yourself.

> **Strength:** I pay my bills on time.
> **Compliment:** I am a responsible money manager.
>
> **Strength:** I pay my credit card balance in full each month, and if I ever find myself unable to do so, I reduce my discretionary expenditures so that I can quickly pay off the bill.
> **Compliment:** I am realistic and the master of my finances.

- **Strength:**

  _____
  _____
  _____

- **Compliment:**

  _____
  _____
  _____

- **Strength:**

  _____
  _____
  _____

- **Compliment:**

  _____
  _____
  _____

- **Strength:**

  _____
  _____
  _____

- **Compliment:**

_____

_____

_____

Keep the list of strengths in a place where you will see it often. Rejoice in your strengths. Relish your ability to compliment yourself.

Do the same exercise with your weaknesses: write the weakness, why you think you do it, and the consequence. Know that in time you can move your weaknesses to the strength page.

Weakness: I never balance my checkbook.
Why I do it: It takes too much of my valuable time.
Consequence: I am never quite sure how much money I have and that worries me.

Weakness: I am borrowing as much money in student loans as I can get.
Why I do it: I want to enjoy life while I am young.
Consequence: I don't know if I will be able to repay the money or not—I may be strapped for money when I graduate and begin paying off my loans.

- **Weakness:**

_____

_____

- **Why I do it:**

_____

_____

- **Consequence:**

_____

_____

_____

- **Weakness:**

_____

_____

_____

- **Why I do it:**

_____

_____

_____

- **Consequence:**

_____

_____

_____

- **Weakness:**

_____

_____

_____

- **Why I do it:**

_____

_____

_____

- **Consequence:**

_____

_____

_____

The path to restructuring your weaknesses into strengths is shaped by taking small steps. It would be nice to resolve all your money problems in one fell swoop, but that is not realistic. Look over your list of weaknesses. Pick the one you fear most, the one that makes your skin prickle when you read it. What is one small thing you could do to deal with this problem? Know that you do not have to solve the problem now. Find one small thing you can do to begin to change this weakness into a strength.

- **My biggest money weakness:**

  _____

  _____

  _____

  _____

  _____

- **One small effort to begin to change:**

  _____

  _____

  _____

  _____

Let's suppose you don't balance your checkbook every month because it takes too much time. Ask yourself why it takes so long. Are you using an ATM every other day for cash? Are you using your debit card for coffee every morning? Do you have so many entries in your checkbook that the sheer act of trying to balance it makes you shut down? If the list of items to reconcile seems overwhelming, what could you do to make it easier? You could go to the ATM once a week and try to operate on cash for incidental purchases such as coffee. This would reduce the entries in your checkbook and speed up the reconciliation process. Resolve to cut down on your checkbook entries for the next month. This is your first small step. Enjoy your progress.

The following month, reconcile your bank account. Don't worry about the previous months of unreconciled statements. Follow the guideline for reconciliation in chapter 4. Write the correct balance in your checkbook. Take a deep breath and enjoy your accomplishment. Now you are ready to balance your checking account every month.

Be creative—look for solutions that suit you. Ask your friends what they do. They may have an answer you have not considered.

Remember that a small step this month can be followed by another small step the next month until you are satisfied that you have conquered the weakness. Just think how easy it is. Within a few months you can move your weakness to your strengths page.

Give yourself time every month to read your strengths and review your progress on your money weaknesses. Perhaps after you pay your bills you reward yourself by reaffirming your strengths. Take a small step every month to master your finances.

LOOK TO THE FUTURE

Take some time to dream. How do you want to leave college? How do you envision your financial situation at graduation? What would be the best, most advantageous position for you to start your professional career? Is this vision achievable?

- **My financial situation at graduation will be**

_____

_____

_____

- **Write down the steps you will take to attain your dream.**

1. _____

_____

_____

2. _____

_____

_____

3. _____

_____

_____

4. _____

_____

_____

5. _____

_____

You have written your own story. You have examined the roots of your relationship with money and reflected on your strengths and weaknesses. Stories are edited and rewritten. Stories evolve. With greater awareness and knowledge over time your money story will change too.

Revisit this chapter at the beginning of each school year. Enjoy the progress you have made in understanding your personal finances and working toward your dreams. Recreate the exercises where you see changes are still needed.

If you can master your finances and money-handling practices while in school, you will have a lifetime of power over money. You will be in charge—you will be a master of your finances.

Glossary of Financial Terms

401(k) plan—a retirement plan funded with the employee's pre-tax dollars. The employer may have an option to match the employee's contribution.

403(b) plan—a tax-sheltered retirement plan for people who work in tax-exempt organizations.

Annual fee—a fee assessed each year by credit card companies. You do not have to write a check for this fee; it is automatically added to your credit card debt. The annual fee is sometimes waived for the first year.

Annual Percentage Rate (APR)—the interest rate you pay expressed as a simple annual percentage. Every lender, including credit card companies, is required to tell you the APR. Always check the APR so you know the interest rate you are paying.

Automated Teller Machine (ATM)—a machine that lets you make cash withdrawals, deposits or transfers between your accounts. If you make withdrawals from an ATM not affiliated with your financial institution, you may be charged a transaction fee.

Bank balance—the amount of money the *bank* shows in an account at a given time. This is not the true balance of your account since there may be checks or deposits that have not yet been processed by the bank.

Bank statement—a list of all the transactions and current balance on a specific account. Usually mailed monthly and often available on-line.

Cancelled check—a check that has been paid and cleared the bank. Can be used as proof of payment and should be kept for a year, if your bank returns cancelled checks with your monthly statement.

Cashier's check—a special type of check issued at your request by a financial institution made payable to a specified receiver. You give the financial institution the money to cover the amount of check, plus a handling fee. A cashier's check guarantees the receiver that funds are available to cover the check.

Certificate of deposit (CD)—a savings device for money deposited in the bank for a fixed amount of time in exchange for a higher interest rate. CDs can be purchased for as little as three months. If you take the money out before the term of the CD, you usually pay a penalty.

Check card—a plastic card that looks like a credit card and works like a check. Be sure to note the amount of the purchase in your check register because the amount is automatically deducted from your checking account. Sometimes called a debit card.

Check register—a journal used to record the checks you write, deposits, fees, ATM withdrawals, and check or debit card transactions. This is where you keep track of all your checking account transactions and your current balance in the account.

Clear—a check has cleared when it has been deducted from your account by your bank.

Collateral—anything of value pledged to a lender until a loan is repaid; e.g., a car is the collateral on an auto loan. Collateral can be seized by the lender if the loan is not paid.

Compound interest—interest earned on principal plus the accumulated interest that was earned earlier. Interest may be calculated daily, monthly, quarterly, or annually. This is why credit card debt is so expensive. You are paying interest on the amount charged plus accumulated interest on the account.

Co-signer—someone who signs a credit agreement along with the borrower. The co-signer is legally obligated to assume responsibility for loan repayment if the borrower doesn't.

Credit bureau—an organization that maintains records on credit and personal financial history. Information is available for a fee to creditors to assess your ability to pay. Can also be accessed by potential employers.

Credit limit—the maximum amount of money you can spend in a credit agreement. Credit cards usually carry a credit limit.

Credit rating—an evaluation of the borrower's credit worthiness and based on the borrowers ability and willingness to pay back loans. Typically devised by a credit bureau or financial institution. See FICO

Creditor—an organization or individual that lends money or to whom money is owed.

Debit card—see check card

Debt—amount(s) you owe and are obligated to pay back, like student loans, credit card charges, and installment loans.

Default—failure to repay a financial obligation according to the terms of the agreement, or failure to submit requests for deferment or cancellation on time. Defaults are registered with credit bureaus, may result in legal action, and may limit future borrowing possibilities.

Deferment—an approved postponement of loan payments for a specific period of time.

Dividends—money paid to a stock shareholder out of a company's earnings.

Endorse—to sign your name on the back of a check that's made out to you. Once you sign the check it is like cash; you can get cash, deposit the money into your account, or sign the check over to someone else. It is best not to endorse a check until you are ready to use it; if you lose the endorsed check someone could cash it and you have no recourse.

Federal direct student loan program (FDSLP, FDSL, FDLP, FDL)—federal loan programs where the student borrows directly from the government.

Federal Educational Loan Program (FELP), Federal Family Education Loan Program (FFELP)—federal loan programs where the student borrows from a commercial lender, but the loans are guaranteed against default by the federal government.

FICO—an acronym for Fair Isaac Corporation, a company that devised the widely used credit risk score model.

Financial aid—the combination of grants, scholarships, work study, and student loans provided by state and federal governments, the school, and private sponsors.

Fixed rate—a rate of interest that does not change over the life of the loan. Other loans may carry a variable interest rate. Always confirm the rate and type of interest when you take out a loan.

Grants—monies awarded a student. Does not need to be repaid.

Gross income—the total amount of money from a job before deductions such as federal, state, city, and social security taxes are taken. Also see net income.

Individual retirement account (IRA)—tax-deferred plan where qualified individuals can set up a retirement account. Contributions and earnings are not taxed until withdrawn at retirement. Penalties are assessed for early withdrawal. Also see Roth IRA.

Installment loan—a loan for a set amount of money that is to be repaid, usually monthly, over a period of time. An automobile loan is an example.

Interest—a fee paid for the use of money. You earn interest by depositing money into an interest-bearing account. You pay interest when you borrow money.

Lease—a contract to rent property.

Loan—money that is borrowed with a formal promise to repay over time with interest.

Money market funds—short term investments that are similar to savings accounts. Usually pay a higher interest rate.

Mutual funds—investment of funds made up of cash and securities and directed by a manager who buys and sells on behalf of investors. Think of it as a big pot where a number of investors pool their money to buy investments.

Net income—often called take-home pay, this is the amount of money you receive from your job after taxes and other deductions are taken from the gross amount.

Non-sufficient funds (NSF)—not enough money in a checking account to cover a check. This is the official name for a "bounced" check. The check will be returned to the person or business trying to cash the check, they will probably be charged a fee, and you will be charged a fee. You will have to make the check good by depositing sufficient funds into your account and having the check redeposited.

Overdraft protection—a line of credit on your checking account that deposits money into your account if you write a check for more than is in the account. Interest, usually at high credit card rates, is charged when this is used. Always have overdraft protection on your checking account.

Payroll deductions—amounts subtracted from your gross pay (federal, state, and city income taxes, health, life, and disability insurance, retirement programs, etc), which results in your net income or take-home pay.

Pell grant—a federal grant for undergraduates based on need.

Perkins loan—a federal low-interest loan based on need for undergraduate and graduate students.

Personal identification number (PIN)—a code you devise to access your accounts. Protect this code information from others.

PLUS loan—a federal loan program for parents. Repayment usually starts after ninety days.

Prime rate—the interest rate that a financial institution charges its best customers.

Principal—the initial amount of a loan before interest is charged. Also, the initial amount of money deposited in an account before interest or dividends are earned.

Reconciliation—to bring into agreement the amount in your bank statement or your check register. This is balancing your bank account.

Renter's insurance—insurance to protect personal property in rental housing such as a dormitory or apartment.

Roth IRA—the initial contribution is made with after-tax dollars, but the earnings are allowed to accumulate without taxes.

Scholarship—financial aid that does not have to be paid back. Sometimes awarded on need, but mostly on personal achievement.

Simple interest—interest charged or interest earned on the principal amount only. It is calculated as principal x interest x time.

Stafford loan—a government student loan. May be subsidized or unsubsidized; i.e., the interest is deferred or starts accruing immediately.

Supplemental Education Opportunity Grant—federal grant awarded to undergraduate students who have exceptional financial need.

Variable rate—an interest rate that can change over time.

W-2 statement—a form that is issued by your employer showing how much you earned in a given calendar year and the payroll tax deductions. Copies of your W-2 form are sent in January to you, and federal, state, and city governments.

W-4 form—a form you fill out for your employer which indicates how many deductions you wish to take. It affects the amount of federal (state) income taxes to be withheld from your paycheck. You should change your W-4 anytime your marital status or dependents change. If you work part-time or only in the summer while a student, you may qualify for an exemption from withholding taxes. Check with your employer.

Work study programs—a federal, need-based program where undergraduate and graduate students can earn a portion of their college expenses through part-time work during the school year.

Index

address, change of, 63–65
allowance, childhood, 123
annual fee, credit card, 91, 133
APR (Annual Percentage Rate), 133
ATM (automated teller machine), 133;
    for account balance, 90; fees, 24,
    39, 43, 133; PIN, 46, 138; using, 24,
    39, 42–43, 44, 129
automobiles. *See* cars

bank accounts: balances of, 134; open-
    ing, 37–38, 39–40; statements for,
    97, 134. *See also* checking accounts;
    savings accounts
bankruptcy, declaring, xi, 55
bills: ignoring, 89–90; learning to pay,
    90, 112; opening, 92; payment
    options for, 77, 93; systems for,
    95–103. *See also* payments
binder system, 101
bonds, 109
borrowing. *See* loans; loans, student
budgets: basics of, 27; cash and, 19,
    24; developing, xi, xii, 15–27; esti-
    mating, 22–23; monitoring, 23, 25;
    parent help with, 15–21, 27; pur-
    poses of, 21; sample, 16–17, 20;

spending plans and, 25, 111–13,
    114

career, 130; choices, 69; start-up costs,
    105–6, 109; wardrobe, 110. *See also*
    jobs
cars: cost of owning, 79–85; leasing,
    86–87; loans for, 50, 59, 68, 72, 74,
    82–83, 85–86, 110–11; parking tick-
    ets on, 80; purchasing, xi
cash: advances, 81, 82; budgets and,
    19, 24; credit cards v., 3, 8, 19, 24;
    emergency, 109; shortage of, 53
cashier's checks, 134
Census Bureau, 2002 report, 36
Certificates of Deposit (CD), 109, 134
charitable contributions, 115–16
checking accounts: ATMs and, 39; bal-
    ancing, 42–43, 47, 50, 75, 76, 89–91,
    96–97, 129, 134, 138; canceled
    checks and, 134; cleared checks
    and, 134; endorsed checks and,
    136; fees, 39, 43, 93; non-sufficient
    funds, 137–38; opening, 37–38,
    39–40; overdraft protection and,
    92–93, 138; register, 134; savings
    accounts v., 18, 24, 51; security,

46–47; signature, 103; stolen checks and, 96–98, 99; understanding, 37–38, 41–46, 75. *See also* bank accounts; debit/check cards
childhood, money and, 123
cleared checks, 134
clothing expenses, 110
collateral, loan, 135
collections office, campus, 61–64
community colleges, 29, 33
compound interest, 135
Consumer Credit Counseling office, 12–13, 14, 55
contracts: auto lease, 86–87, 100; housing rental, 49
co-signing loans, 50, 135
cost of living, 108
credit bureau, 135
credit cards: annual fee on, 3, 91, 133; APR for, 133; basics of, 13–14; cash advances on, 81, 82; cash v., 3, 8, 19, 24; Consumer Credit Counseling for, 12–13, 14, 55; controlling, xii; credit limit on, 8, 11, 13, 14, 66, 74, 91, 135; credit rating and, 2, 11–12, 74, 135; debit/check cards v., 3, 4, 6, 56, 76, 134; debt from, xi, 1–14, 53, 77, 92, 105, 106, 107, 133; freezing, 8–9; help with, 12–13, 14; interest on, 2–4, 53, 74–75, 81–82; late fees on, 91; late payments on, 91; managing/paying off, 4–5, 7–11, 75–76, 81–83; parent advice on, 4, 81–82; security for, 44, 102, 103; seduction by, 1–14, 53; statements for, 102; theft of, 102; usefulness of, 13. *See also* debt
credit history: basics, 78; credit rating and, 2, 11–12, 74, 135; establishing, 4, 11–12, 13, 40, 70–78; impact of, 70–82; negative, 70–73, 75, 77–78; strong, 78
credit reports, 73; clearing, 71–72; organizations providing, 71, 102; requesting, 71, 72
credit unions, 110–11
creditor, 135

debit/check cards, 39, 134; credit cards v., 3, 46, 56, 98, 134
debt, 135; collection agencies, 61, 63; monthly payments for, 59, 66–67, 111; overextending, 54, 61–69; paying off, 53, 55, 78, 81; safe level of, xii, 111. *See also* credit cards; loans; loans, student
default, 135–36
deferment, loan, 135–36
depression, help for, 12
disclosure, marriage and, 54–55, 77–78, 112
dividends, stock, 13
documents, financial: protecting, 98–99; saving/storing, 100–101
donations, charitable, 115–16
Dunn, Lucia, 10–11

education, funding. *See* financial aid; grants; loans, student; scholarships
The Education Research Institute (TERI), 30
emergency funds: personal, 84, 108–9, 113; university, 53, 80, 81, 82
emotions, 83, 100, 116–17
employment. *See* career; jobs
endorse, 136
Equifax, 71, 102
exercises, money, 120–31
expenses: clothing, 111; estimating, 22–23; monitoring, 23, 25; monthly living, 68–69, 105–6, 107; post-college, 104–13
Experian, 68, 102

Fair Isaac Corporation. *See* FICO
family: influence, 120–23; loans, 111
fathers, influence of, 4–5, 121–22
Federal Direct Student Loan Program (FDSLP), 136
Federal Education Loan Program (FELP), 136
fee collection office, campus, 97
females, influence of, 120–21
FICA (Social Security), 67

FICO (Fair Isaac Corporation), 136
filing systems, 95–103
financial aid, 28–36, 136; applying for, 30–31, 35; basics, 31–33, 36; collections office, 61–64; offices/officers, 12, 34, 54, 61. *See also* grants; loans, student; scholarships
fixed rate interest, 136
401(k) plans, 106, 133
403(k) plans, 133
friends, influence of, 122–23
furniture needs, 110
future: financial basics for, 113; looking to, 106–7, 112, 130–31; money, spending, 57; visualizing, 59, 130

giving, financial, 114–15
graduate school loans, 82
graduation: finances at, 130; planning for after, 104–13
grants, 29, 31–32, 136; federal, 32, 138, 139; Pell, 32, 138; state, 32; Supplemental Education Opportunity, 139; work-study, 32
gratitude, lessons of, 114–15, 119
gross income, 137

Habitat for Humanity, 115
help: asking for, 50; budget, 15–21, 27; credit card, 12–13, 14; for depression, 12; spending, 56

identity theft, 101–2
income: gross, 137; monthly take-home, 66–67, 105, 113; net, 137; payroll deductions from, 138
income taxes. *See* taxes
individual retirement accounts. *See* IRAs
injuries, 109
installment loans, 137
insurance: disability, 108, 113; documents, 100; health/medical, xi, 48, 67, 107, 113; parents' homeowners, 48; renter's, xi, 49, 51, 138
interest rates, 137; APR, 133; compound interest and, 135; credit card, 2–4, 53, 74–75, 76, 81–82; fixed, 136; negotiating, 74–75; overdraft protection and, 93, 138; prime, 71–72, 136; simple, 139; student loan, 64–65; variable, 139
IRAs (individual retirement accounts), 105, 135; Roth, 105, 137

jobs: cooperative programs for, 33–34; to pay off debts, 53, 55, 80, 81; while in school, 32, 33–34, 80, 139; work-study for, 32, 139. *See also* career

leases, 47–48, 139; car, 86–87, 100; rental, 48–49, 51, 137
living: cost of, 20, 25, 108; expenses, 68–69, 105–6, 109
loans, 137; agreements, 100; amortization, 111; car, 26, 36, 50, 59, 68, 72, 82–83, 86, 110–11; collateral, 135; co-signing, 50, 135; credit union, 110–11; default, 135–36; deferment, 135, 136; evaluation, 85; family, 111; installment, 137; Perkins, 138; principal, 138; repayment of, 111; to/from friends, 50; total monthly payments for, 59, 62, 66–68, 105, 111. *See also* debt
loans, student, xii, 15–17, 29, 82; basics, 69; charity v., 35; collections, 61–64; federal, 32–33, 64, 136, 139; graduate school, 82–83; interest, 64–65; Inventory Master List worksheet, 65–68; keeping track of, 58–59, 64–67; Loan Summary worksheet, 59, 65–66; looking for, 30–31; monthly living expenses and, 68; monthly take-home pay and, 67; packages, 32; parent/PLUS, 33, 138; Perkins, 32, 139; repayment, 35–36, 54–55, 58–59, 60, 62, 64; Stafford, 32, 33, 139; subsidized v. unsubsidized, 32–33, 139. *See also* debt; financial aid

long-term investments, 109
lump sum payments, 37, 48

mail, opening, 92, 94
males, influence of, 120–21
marriage, finances and, 54–55, 77–78, 112
Medicare, 67
mellow, being, 116–17, 118
Microsoft Money, 77, 112
military academies, 33
money management: options, 23–24, 92; questions, 120–31
money market funds, 109, 137
monthly: living expenses, 67–69, 105, 109; payment totals, 59, 62, 66–68, 105, 111; savings, 108–9; take-home pay, 67, 69, 111, 116
mothers, influence of, 15–20, 120–21
mutual funds, 137

nest eggs, 118
net income, 137
non-sufficient funds (NSF), 137–38

online banking, 39; bill payment, 77, 92, 94
organizational systems, 95–103
overdraft protection, 39, 72, 92–93, 138

Parent Loan for Undergraduate Students (PLUS). *See* PLUS loans
parents: borrowing by, 33; budget advice from, 15–21, 27; credit card advice from, 4, 81–82; family loans from, 111; financial responsibility advice from, 89–90; homeowners insurance of, 48; influence of male/female, 120–21; PLUS loans for, 33, 138; vital information list to, 101
parking tickets, 80, 84, 87
pay. *See* income
payments: automatic, 94; giving thanks and, 114–15, 118; late,

70–71, 73, 75, 89–90, 91–92; lump sum, 37, 48; online, 77, 91, 94; options for, 77, 92. *See also* bills
payroll deductions, 138
Pell grants, 32, 138
Perkins loans, 32, 139
personal identification number. *See* PIN
philosophy, personal money, 114–19
"pile" system, 95–97, 98, 100
PIN (personal identification number): ATM card, 47, 138; securing, 101
planning, post-college, 104–13
PLUS loans (Parent Loan for Undergraduate Students), 33, 138
prime rate, 74–75, 138
principal, loan/account, 138
procrastination, 89–92
prosperous, feeling, 117–18, 119
purchases, basics for, 87

questions, money, 120–31
Quicken, 77, 112

receipts, saving, 100
reconciliation, 138
register, check, 134
rental housing: contracts, 48–49; credit history impact on, 70–71
renter's insurance, 49, 51, 138
responsibility, financial: basics of, 93–94; ignoring, 88–94
retirement programs: 401(k), 106, 133; 403(k), 133; contributing to, 106, 113; IRA, 107–8, 137; Roth IRA, 107, 139
role models, 123
ROTC scholarships, 33

safe deposit boxes, 101
salary. *See* income
savings accounts: balances of, 134; checking accounts v., 18, 24, 51; emergency funds and, 83, 113; monthly savings for, 108–9; nest eggs and, 118; opening, 48

scholarships, 29, 31, 139; ROTC, 33; website for, 31. *See also* financial aid

security: basics, 103; checking account, 46; credit card, 46, 102, 103; document, 98–101; identity theft,101–2

sharing, financial, 115–16

sibling influence on money management, 122

simple interest, 139

social security number, 98, 101, 102, 103

software: Microsoft Money, 77, 112; personal accounting, 15, 17–18, 23, 77, 101, 112; Quicken, 77, 112; spreadsheet programs, 23

spending: basics, 60, 87; controlling, 5–6, 26, 52–60, 74; diversity in, 112; post-college, 104–13; triggers, 74

spending plans. *See* budgets

spreadsheet programs, 23

Stafford loans, 32, 33, 139

stocks, 109; dividends from, 136

storage, document, 101

story, writing own money, 120–31

strengths/weaknesses, financial, 125–30, 131

student loans. *See* loans, student

suicide, 12

Supplemental Education Opportunity Grant, 139

systems, file, 95–103

taxes: deductions and, 139; federal income, 49, 63, 67, 139; FICA (Social Security), 67; keeping documents for, 100; Medicare, 67; state income, 67

theft, 103; credit card, 102; identity, 101–2; stolen checks as, 97–99

TransUnion, 68, 100

Treasury bills, 109

unemployment, 109

variable rate interest, 139

volunteering, 115–16

W-2 statements, 59, 100, 139

W-4 form, 139

wardrobe, career, 110

warranties, saving, 100

weaknesses/strengths, financial, 125–30, 131

websites: loan amortization, 111; scholarship, 31

wish-list cards, 105–6, 109–10

working. *See* career; jobs

work-study programs, 32, 139

About the Author

Susan Knox is a CPA, financial planner, and has a long association with higher education. She taught accounting at Franklin University of Columbus, Ohio and spent ten years as an administrator at The Ohio State University. As associate treasurer, Susan had the responsibility for student aid accounting, student loan collections, fees and deposits, systems developments, cash management, and short-term investments. As assistant to the provost she had budgetary responsibility to eighteen colleges within the university.

Susan left Ohio State to start her own CPA firm specializing in personal financial planning and taxes. She received a Certificate in Educational Achievement for personal Financial Planning from the American Institute of Certified Public Accountants.

After moving to the Pacific Northwest, Susan turned her attention to writing. She lives in Seattle with her husband, just north of the Pike Place Market, where she enjoys a view of Elliot Bay and the gustatory riches of the market where she shops daily. She is the mother/stepmother of four children who no longer live at home, but who encourage their mom to write and to share her wisdom.

Susan believes that the experience she has gained as a financial planner, educator, and writer translate well into the content and tone of *Financial Basics*. She encourages readers of this book to send comments and suggestions to susan@financialbasics.org, and she has provided a website with blank worksheets at www.financialbasics.org.